THE WOMAN'S BOOK *of*
MONEY *&*
SPIRITUAL VISION

THE WOMAN'S BOOK *of* MONEY *&* SPIRITUAL VISION

Putting Your Spiritual Values into Financial Practice

ROSEMARY WILLIAMS

with Joanne Kabak

New World Library
Novato, California

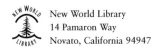 New World Library
14 Pamaron Way
Novato, California 94947

Book design by Madonna Gauding

Library of Congress Cataloging-in-Publication Data
Williams, Rosemary, date.
The woman's book of money & spiritual vision : putting your financial
values into spiritual practice / Rosemary Williams with Joanne Kabak.
— Rev. and upd. ed.
p. cm.
ISBN 978-1-880913-67-3 (pbk.)
Originally published: Philadelphia : Innisfree Press, ©2001.
Includes worksheets, journaling exercises and meditations.
1. Women—Finance, Personal. 2. Finance, Personal—Religious
aspects—Christianity. 3. Spirituality. I. Kabak, Joanne, date.
II. Title. III. Woman's book of money and spiritual vision.
HG179 .W55 2005
332.024/0082—dc22 0511

ISBN 978-1-880913-67-3

 New World Library is a proud member of the Green Press Initiative.

10   9   8   7   6   5   4   3   2

To my mother, Teresa Cullen, and my friend Dr. Ida F. Davidoff, two important women in my life who offered me examples of courage, understanding, and love. I also dedicate this book to the many women who infuse my life today with their dreams and perseverance and use their energies for the greater good.

—Rosemary Williams

In memory of my sister Irene (1942-2001), who was always the loving big sister in the wild ride of childhood and womanhood. She encouraged me to write, and her pride in my work knew no bounds.

—Joanne Kabak

Contents

Gratitudes

In writing this book, I am especially grateful to Inner Ocean Publishing for the invitation to create a new edition and to Innisfree Press for inviting me to write the book initially. There are many people who have been directly involved in this project and to whom I feel much gratitude. I thank my collaborator, Joanne Kabak, who is a joy to work with and who has put my ideas into the written word for both editions. A special thank you to Karen Bouris, Alma Bune, and Angela Watrous for their oversight of the manuscript and to Charyn Atkin for designing the new cover. I remain grateful to Marcia Broucek, Marjory Bankson, and Ruth Butler, who supported the creation of this book from the very beginning and to all those who opened their hearts and let their stories be told. I thank Jean Shinoda Bolen for lighting my way with her example of giving a strong public voice to her thoughts. Jean added the term "divine assignment" to my vocabulary. I believe this book is one of my divine assignments.

In addition, I am very grateful to the many, many people who have influenced this book. It would be impossible to name them all for they include my family, friends, colleagues, clients, coworkers, and fellow seekers who have supported me throughout my life. I look forward to continuing on the journey with them, and with all those who are seeking to align their financial life with their spiritual vision.

—ROSEMARY WILLIAMS

As the collaborator on this book, I want to express my great joy in working with Rosemary and my gratitude for her trusting me to help carry her message to a wider world through the printed word. Thanks to my husband and daughters for their love and for tiptoeing by the computer while I'm at work—even on a holiday weekend!

I would like to thank the brilliant newspaper editor Joyce Gabriel, who had the courage to create seminars to teach women about money at a time when this was a unique mission. Her work brought Rosemary and me together. I would also like to thank the women who are part of the different spiritual, entrepreneurial, and writers' groups I belong to. They feed my soul, critique my words, and help me make a living!

—JOANNE KABAK

A New Beginning

My prayer for *The Woman's Book of Money and Spiritual Vision.*

May the ideas in this book become readily available to you and to many other women.

May the words open your heart, give no offense, and expand your vision to all possibility.

May you find a deep, underlying peace and an integrated life.

May the book encourage you to unite the powers of money and spirit so they work in tandem, shifting economic systems to serve the greater good rather than to benefit the few.

May the rich, the poor, and those in the middle come to know and understand each other in an honest and enduring way.

May people of all economic levels share their feelings and eliminate the artificial sense of separation based on financial distinctions.

May no one be made invisible or taken advantage of based on whether they have much or little.

May the isolation that comes from not having enough money as well as the isolation that comes from having more than enough money disappear through a sense of unity and the recognition that we are all members of one family.

May this book feed the soul of everyone who works with it in any way and those who become beneficiaries of its concepts.

Introduction

> To view the use of money as a spiritual practice is to create an engaged, embodied spirituality. It is to live out your spiritual truth on a daily basis, in all of your day-to-day transactions.

*T*his book is a very different look at money, one that I hope will change your life. The work I am asking you to do is not just about organizing your finances better—though you will learn how to do so. Nor is it about ways to contribute more for the good of others—though you will surely be encouraged to do so.

This "workshop in a book" is designed to change your way of looking at money—to shift your perspective from a material base to a spiritual base, from consumption to generosity, from bettering your own world to bettering everyone's world. The spirituality expressed in this book is based on my belief that a part of each of us transcends the human plane. This transcendent consciousness is what I call spirituality. It is our core, our center, our commonality. I do believe the human species is one family, united by spirit. Having a Jewish/Catholic heritage and being part of an interfaith community, I have come to realize that a universal spirit exists that is bigger than any one religion. This book is written with the goal of being inclusive of all spiritual belief systems whether defined as religious or not. I believe in a benign spiritual power that includes all peoples, all cultures, and all disciplines. Words cannot capture or describe it.

My hope for this book is that as you do the exercises and read the stories, you will experience your own spirituality, acknowledge it as an active principle in your life, and feel inspired to infuse your economic decisions with your spiritual vision. I cannot say exactly how this transformation will unfold for you because I believe each of us has our own distinct path to walk. It is by reflecting on the messages, history, facts, and dreams of your own life that you will be able to use the resources available to you to consciously and intentionally walk the path and take the actions that will move you forward, uniting your economic and spiritual power.

Money and spirituality need not be mutually exclusive. I believe there is a spiritual dimension to money that can be tapped for your benefit—and for global benefit—and this book is directed toward that end. The transformation comes about from cultivating awareness, acceptance, and action. It starts when you make a commitment to understanding your personal financial facts and uncovering the feelings that these facts bring up. And it continues with your ongoing efforts to align these facts and feelings with your core desires and intentions.

At certain points along the road of your life, your financial and spiritual aspects touch each other in a very direct way. At other times, they run parallel to one another. But they are never far apart, even if your awareness is not specifically drawn to them.

In the five years since I first began writing a book about women, money, and spirituality, I have worked with thousands of women of all economic levels and age ranges, in meetings, conferences, and workshops in the United States and other countries. I am always asking, "Where does your financial life intersect with your spiritual life? Do you ever connect your use of money to your soul?" Most often, I get a blank stare in response. "What do you mean?" most people reply. While I see a very natural connection between money and spirituality, many others do not. Therein lies the work of this book—to connect the dots, to make the links, to develop a clear understanding of how the power of money illustrates and magnifies our individual core values and spirituality.

Perhaps if I share part of my story with you, I can illustrate what I mean. As is true for many women, pain and necessity have often been my teachers and have forced me to change. During a time of downsizing and bank mergers in New England in the early nineties, I lost my job as a banker. I opened a financial planning practice on my own and later joined a friend who was also a financial planner. At this time I was introduced to the Ministry of Money and Women's Perspective. The Ministry of Money is an organization based in Germantown, Maryland, that for nearly thirty years has provided opportunities for people to explore their relationship to money from a Christian perspective. Women's Perspective, which originated from the Ministry of Money, is now a separate, nonsectarian organization based in Fairfield, Connecticut, that provides opportunities for women to explore their relationship with money from a spiritual perspective.

The idea of seeing money through a spiritual lens was compelling to me. I went to a few Ministry of Money workshops, volunteered as a workshop facilitator with this organization, and became more and more interested in the work it was doing. The director invited me to accompany him and a few board members to Haiti for three days. When I asked, "Why?" he replied, "I'd like to introduce you to some people there and to what we are doing there."

That simple invitation to Haiti changed my life and became the inspiration for my future work. Visiting Haiti gave me the opportunity to experience an underdeveloped, economically deprived, financially handicapped, nonconsumer culture with a deep sense of community and an ordinary practice of generosity. My heart exploded open and I knew I had much to learn from the Haitian people about living, loving, and caring for one another. I also had much to learn about the economic interdependence of countries in our rapidly changing global economy. I am now the director of Women's Perspective, which has become an independent, nonprofit educational organization. I am deeply committed to creating workshops for women and sustaining the women's programs we initiated in Haiti and Kenya. We will continue to find ways to improve the lives of people we meet in economically deprived countries on a scale that is small but empowering. I am following a call that brings me face to face with global economics: at the United Nations, where I have joined with women delegates from all over the world at meetings of the Committee on the Status of Women and with representatives of the world's religions at the NGO Committee on Spirituality, Values, and Global Concerns.

I made the personal journey of evolution from obedient Catholic, dutiful daughter, and suburban housewife, first to becoming a full-time financial planner and breadwinner, then a catalyst for helping women from around the world transform their relationship with money. My trips, events, and meetings have put me in contact with women from varied economic, cultural, ethnic, and faith backgrounds who have shared their stories with me. My understanding of spirituality and economics has broadened beyond any of my expectations. The box that once contained my life has enlarged well beyond my original imaginings. Still, I remain a work in progress, continuing to realize the enormity of the spiritual context of our world. As my awareness grows, so does my desire to bring other women into ways of expanding their worlds. I do this with conviction because I know that, in this process, I have arrived at a fuller version of womanhood and personhood. And I do it because I have experienced the peace that comes with living a life expressed through work that matters.

Sometimes a simple invitation can change your life.

Now I invite you to follow the money through reading and doing the exercises in this book.

An Invitation to "Follow the Money"

"Follow the money" sounds like such a harsh command. It's one that very few women are ever given as young girls, or indeed at any point in their lives. But it's advice that I encourage you to take throughout this book. First follow the money with attention to the details of your own accounts. Then follow the trail of where money goes in the wider world as well. Start to think about questions such as: "Where does this money go?" "Who benefits?" "What is the ultimate message of money?" Bring these questions into your spiritual practice and your consciousness about money.

I ask you to look at where your money comes from, where it is right now, where it goes, and how and why it leaves you. I ask you to follow the money through the messages you've received, through your own personal history, and through your checkbook and bank statements. I ask you to follow the money right out your door, into your career and your life activities, and all the way into your dreams about what you really want to be doing with your gifts, talents, hours, and days

I am glad that you are joining me in this process of self-discovery and have decided to look at the relationship between two of the most important aspects of your life at the same time: your money and your spirituality. *The Woman's Book of Money and Spiritual Vision* offers tools to help you explore and examine how you relate to money and how money connects to your faith, your spiritual beliefs, your value system, and your relationship to yourself and your sense of the divine.

Now that you hold this book in your hands, I invite you to prepare yourself for the adventure of exploring your own personal beliefs and behaviors. Think about this possibility: Reading this book about money at *this* time in your life may be part of the divine architecture of your life, just as writing it is part of mine. Once you can begin to accept that the timing is right for you to do this, you can see it as the beginning of transformational work.

I am experiencing the revision of this book as my divine assignment, using the gifts of attunement and meditation I have learned at Findhorn, a forty-year-old spiritual community in Scotland; through meditation at Gampo Abbey, a Buddhist center in Nova Scotia; and from Marilyn Clements, a meditation teacher and visual artist who describes a meditation method called "Self-Attunement." My early Christian training, which taught me, "Ask and you shall receive," plays a strong role in my life as well. Faith in a power I cannot see but can deeply feel has been a constant part of my life and carries me along my path. These disciplines are what I call on as I write this revision.

To help you access your own spiritual core, as you begin your work on money and spirituality I recommend you set aside time to quiet yourself, allowing inspiration, meditation, and prayer to calm and center you, making these rituals a part of the time you spend on this work.

By going through the exercises in this book, you can align your financial beliefs with your spiritual values. You can take control of your finances so you don't squander, waste, or give up control of your money. And you can do so without sacrificing what you really want to do in life, what you feel at the deepest levels to be your purpose in life.

I hope this experience will be transformative and freeing for you, that it will open doors to new ways of seeing, believing, and doing.

These are the kinds of questions I will be asking you to consider along the way:

- **Am I a generous person?**

- **How do I give to myself?**

- **How do I give my time, my possessions, my money to others?**

- **How much are my economic transactions influenced by my values? How much are they motivated by habit?**

Use this book as your personal diary: write in it, scribble notes in the margins, let it capture your ideas and insights. You may also want to record your thoughts in a journal or a notebook. The medium doesn't matter, but the message does. Express your reactions, positive or negative, because both contain valuable insights. There is no formula you must follow other than to record your responses and observations for future reflection.

Consider embarking on this spiritual money journey with a group of women or at least one other woman. While this book is your guide, other people can be your coaches in this endeavor. By gathering together, you give each other incentive and encouragement to complete the process and take the next step. If you decide to share your experiences as a group, it will be helpful to establish some basic ground rules for your time together, such as agreeing to be open with each other and to hold the information you share in confidentiality.

Of course it is also useful to do this work alone. Your challenge will be to be honest with yourself about the subject of finances and to encourage yourself along the way.

A Quick Inventory

Before you go further, I am going to ask you to take a few minutes to complete the following quick inventory of how you currently understand your financial life.

1. My financial life is:

___ in order

___ could use some work

___ a mess

___ a catastrophe

___ being taken care of by someone else

___ other _____

2. My financial facts are:

___ clear to me

___ readily available

___ confusing

___ unknown

___ missing

___ other _____

3. When I consider my financial life, I feel:

___ ready to know more

___ open to some input

___ secure

___ calm

___ embarrassed

___ overwhelmed

___ confused

___ scared

___ angry

___ other _____

4. When I consider my spiritual life:

___ I believe there is a Divinity.

___ I feel very removed from the idea of Divinity.

___ I'm not sure what I believe.

___ other _____

5. I spend time in prayer or meditation:

___ daily

___ frequently

___ once in a while

___ hardly ever

6. I would describe my spiritual life as:

___ active

___ burgeoning

___ stuck

___ dormant

___ more of a "sometimes" thing

___ transitioning

___ unable to describe

7. Conclude your personal inventory by answering the question, What does money mean to me? Jot down what comes to mind first, without analyzing or judging your immediate responses.

Money means . . .

To be poor means . . .

To be rich means . . .

To have enough means . . .

When I share what I have, I feel . . .

Every Possibility

Margaret J. Wheatley, author of *Leadership and the New Sciences*, tells us, "There is only what we create through our engagement with others and with events. Nothing really transfers; everything is always new and different and unique to each of us. Reality depends upon your engagement."

I hope your engagement with this book brings new insights and a respect for the power of your beliefs in combination with the power of your resources. Read it with the intention to change, for every possibility is open to you.

Read with the intention to change, for every possibility is open to you.

Chapter One

Your Money Messages

The King was in the counting house
counting out his money.
The Queen was in the parlor
eating bread and honey.

—*Sing a Song of Sixpence*

*A*s many times as a child that I recited these lines from "Sing a Song of Sixpence," I never imagined that they would pop into my head forty years later at the precise moment they were most applicable.

Yet there I was, the only woman and newest member of the private banking department of a large commercial bank, sitting at a conference table with seven men in an elegant cherry-paneled board room. The vice president expounded on the new marketing plan for several minutes before he turned to the group and asked, "Does anyone have a comment?"

A few of the men murmured some compliments, and then I spoke up. I believed I had an important point to make, an enhancement to the plan. So I expressed it. My words then hung in the air and echoed in the room. Silence. Dead silence.

It became very clear to me that I was not expected to say anything. My words were simply ignored, and the men continued the conversation as if no one had spoken. And all I could think of, as I observed the faces around the table, was that in this bank conference room the "King" was in charge of the money. And the "Queen" was to have no part of it.

the
money
journey
circle

"*To undo our very ancient and very stuck habitual patterns of mind requires that we begin to turn around some of our most basic assumptions.*"

—PEMA CHODRON,
When Things Fall Apart

Money Is Never Neutral

Money never seems to be neutral. It has an emotional overlay that contains the attitudes of our parents, our friends, our religious institutions, and our culture. The power of what we have been taught can pop up at any moment, in decisions large and small. These are what I call "money messages." Our money messages create a system of beliefs that become the rudder of our economic lives for good or for ill. Money messages enter into the activities of the present, turning yesterday's ideas into the driving force for today's actions.

The message I had received from the nursery rhyme was, "Keep quiet about money matters because men deal with money and women don't." Sure, I might make a simple suggestion, or ask a question when appropriate, but I normally did not argue for my point of view. Then when I did express my opinion in the bank's high-level environment—*wham!*—I was hit with the message to be quiet again. (I guess the others in the room had heard the same rhyme, too, or a similar one. No one acted in a way that showed they believed I had the right to speak or be acknowledged!)

"Events of our earliest years establish patterns of thinking, feeling, and acting that influence us for a lifetime."
—Victor Daniels and Laurence J. Horowitz,
Being and Caring

My messages about money contain the attitudes of my mother, my grandmother, and other family members from both sides. But that's not all. They also contain the history of my life, the information I've absorbed from home, school, church, movies, music, magazines, and friendships. And so do yours.

Money Myths Always Show Up

Sometimes money messages come to light in surprising moments. Once when talking about money messages with a friend of mine who is a successful attorney, she disagreed with me about the role of unconscious agendas: "I don't think I fall prey to any of that. I am so analytical. I think everything through, and go over and over the details until I come to a clear decision."

We happened to be sitting in her living room, which was filled with books and bookshelves. In fact, she had so many books, she had added extra shelves in the dining room and over the door jamb. As she sat back to think about what she had just said, she glanced around the room and started smiling. The smile spread across her whole face, and she laughed out loud.

Money messages contain the attitudes of your mother, your grandmother, and other family members—as well as information from school, church, movies, music, magazines, and friendships.

"Okay, okay," she said. "I see what you mean. I am analytical about everything except books. And do you want to know why? When I was a young girl, my father would give me an allowance and say, 'Spend your money wisely. Do not be frivolous and buy things you don't need. But books, books are not frivolous. Always surround yourself with good books.' And look at what I've done, without even realizing it. I am surrounded by good books!"

Money messages are different for each of us, though many of us have absorbed similar ones, bound as we are by our generation and our ethnic or geographic origins. Usually the money story we live by is inherited. It may be generations old—and the strength of our ties to this history may bind us in ways that we aren't conscious of—but the story we learn keeps unfolding over time. What we are taught will show up in some way!

In my household, as in many others, when I was growing up, money was a private affair. It was a family matter, never to be discussed outside the house—and, sometimes, not even inside it! Girls, especially, were often told not to ask questions about how much things cost or not to "worry your pretty head about that." As if "that" were a taboo subject.

During a workshop I was presenting on the subject of money messages, one woman in the group, who was the manager of special project funds for her religious organization, stood up and said, "Stop! I just had a flashback. I saw my mother putting my father's weekly salary in envelopes labeled for all our expenses."

She went on to say, "Do you know I have set up the accounts in the same way? Now I understand why I have such a difficult time saying yes to anyone who comes to me for funds for a new project.

It is simply not on the books. There is not a category for it! No envelope! My mother would say no to new things because the money was always already distributed in the envelopes. It was all accounted for beforehand. There was no room for creativity or discussion."

Money was originally designed to be an economic tool, but in our society it has come to represent much more than a means of exchanging goods and services. I'm asking you to consider how aware you are of the emotional overtones of your money—whether it is earned, inherited, won, given as allowance, or received as a gift or in the settlement of a dispute.

The First Stage of Your Money Journey

The diagram on the facing page depicts the six stages of The Money Journey Circle that you will be working with in this book. The first stage, *Money Messages*, involves uncovering the messages that have been implanted in your unconscious. This is the stage of awareness, of understanding the money mythology you have believed in and have lived out, often without even knowing what you were doing.

"Once I became aware of money messages, I began to recognize them more and more. They appeared at unexpected times in the course of my day. I would get an 'aha' moment and see that I was making an automatic choice from an old message!"

—A WORKSHOP PARTICIPANT

It is critically important to identify the messages that influence your financial actions, but the subtle "rules" you live by may be hard to uncover because they are so deeply embedded. That is why I suggest that you write down your thoughts and responses as we take this money journey together. This will give you a chance to step back and examine how these themes affect your current life and to gain more understanding of the power these messages have on your behavior.

The process starts with exploring how you learned about money. I believe that nothing in life, including the messages you heard in nursery rhymes or parental admonitions, is inconsequential, extraneous, or wasted. The exercises in this chapter will help you uncover those money messages and use that

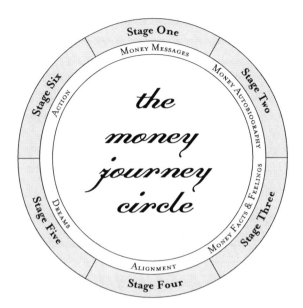

Stage One, *Money Messages:*
The myths about money you grew up with, believe in, and live out.

Stage Two, *Money Autobiography:*
The story of your experiences and relationships with money.

Stage Three, *Money Facts and Feelings:*
The uncovering of your financial facts and how you feel about them.

Stage Four, *Alignment:*
The integration of your facts, feelings, and actions with your spiritual core.

Stage Five, *Dreams:*
The exploration of your call.

Stage Six, *Action:*
The plan.

information as the starting point not only to get a grip on your finances but also to go forward, and inward, to the spiritual connection to money.

I will be asking you to remember, imagine, write, examine, evaluate, listen to stories, and acknowledge *the story you learned about money*. It will then be up to you to decide if you want to keep your myth or to develop a new story that is compatible with the way you want to live your life now.

Perhaps if I share more of my life story with you, I can illustrate what I mean. I am a white, North American woman who grew up in the Northeast as the only child of a widow in a middle-class family. I was raised Catholic and influenced by my deceased father's Jewish family. I went to a Catholic high school and college. As a college student, and later as the wife of a young corporate executive, living in suburban Connecticut and raising five children, I was locked into a set of beliefs and attitudes that kept my world in a very small box. The outlines of that box were drawn by color, genes, geographic location, class, religion, education, and marriage, along with many other more minor details.

After my divorce, my life changed, and so did the outlines of my box. I was now a single parent who cared for my children while I worked as a banker, financial planner, and consultant to nonprofit organizations. I interacted daily with people and their money. In this role I gained new perspective. As I observed others making financial decisions, I noticed that they—and I—always wanted more of everything and that most of us were never satisfied. The annual raise or the bonus always brought with it new desires and needs.

As I began to work with my own new awareness and to question others about their money motives, I found we had much in common. I also began to notice people behaving in ways that did not seem connected to their current financial circumstances. I began to recognize that "money messages" always make an appearance—with an intensely personal agenda.

When I recognized one of my own myths, I realized I no longer wanted to be the "Queen" who was not allowed to think, speak, or deal with money. I replaced this myth with a new, ever-evolving story, one that I will share with you throughout this book

Now it is time to explore your own money messages, myths, and stories.

A Prayer for the Journey

May I find:

◆ **Courage to examine my financial life.**

◆ **Perseverance to uncover the messages that have shaped my thinking**

◆ **Strength to merge the beliefs of my soul with the reality of my money.**

◆ **Wisdom to understand what true wealth is and how to use it.**

Family Patterns

The process of uncovering money messages takes time. Remember, you are developing a composite view of yourself and your belief system.

This first set of questions will help you identify the family money patterns you experienced as you were growing up. Again and again, in workshops and individual discussions, I have seen revelations emerge as women have answered the eight questions that follow. Answer each question as honestly as you can, remembering that there is no right or wrong answer. There is only the opportunity to increase awareness of your thinking patterns, your attitudes, and your motivations.

1. **When you were growing up, who handled the money in your family?** Who made the major financial decisions?

2. **How were money decisions or problems handled?** Was money discussed openly ? Who was a part of the discussion?

3. **Describe how you saw a major financial decision being made.**

4. **Did you think that the money available in your household was scarce or abundant?** What did you hear or see that created this perception?

5. **When you look back, do you think your perception of the money supply at home was accurate?** Was your perception the result of your own observation or based on what some one else told you?

6. **Do you remember how you actually felt about money as a child?** Write a sentence or two describing your feelings.

7. **Describe a childhood experience related to money that has stayed in your mind.**

8. **What feelings surface for you when you think of the money history of your family?**

Following are some common examples of money messages. You may want to circle those messages that you've been exposed to, and perhaps add them to your money journal:

- ◆ Be grateful for what you have.

- ◆ Do you think we're made of money?

- ◆ There is not enough money, but don't let anyone know.

- Don't tell people how much money you make.

- Don't take any wooden nickels.

- People with money are better than us.

- People who don't have money aren't as good as us.

- You should only buy things on sale.

- You should always save your money.

- Do you think money grows on trees?

- There is always enough money to go around.

- Don't be wasteful.

- Make do with what you have.

- When we were kids, we didn't spend money like that.

- Do you know how much it costs to heat the house?

- We have to keep up with the Joneses.

- Everything costs money.

- Don't marry someone who doesn't make enough to take care of you.

- You have no concept of money.

- A penny saved is a penny earned.

- A penny saved is a penny.

- Beware the almighty dollar.

- Starving people in Russia/China/etc. would love to have what you have.

- Sometimes things are worth spending money on.

- You should be a teacher so you can have summers off.

- Money is not for girls, the men take care of it.

- A family's money should be reserved for the boys' education. You'll always be taken care of—you don't have to worry.

- What makes you think you can do what you want?

- If you buy it, let it be quality.

- We are lucky.

- I owe my parents for working hard to financially support me.

- Never make long-distance calls.

- I don't remember worrying about money or feeling deprived.

- People with money are important.

- Without money, life is difficult.

- Save your best things for when we have company.

- Don't act poor. People will look down on you.

- Save and don't spend needlessly.

- There isn't enough to go around.

- Save for a rainy day.

- Find a career that will give you security (even if you don't like it).

- Do you think we are made of money?

- It is easier for a camel to go through the eye of a needle than for a rich man to enter heaven.

- Money comes from God with the implication that He can take it away and there's nothing you can do to earn it.

- It was wrong to take a job you didn't need to support yourself. It was taking food out of someone's mouth.

- Never ask for things. Wait until they're offered.

- You'll have to work to help support the family.

- The check hasn't come from the government yet. Make do.

- We can't afford it.

- You have the golden touch!

- Money is an agreed-upon illusion.

- We work hard so our kids will have what we didn't have.

- You should never pay someone to do something you're capable of doing yourself.

- Why not pay someone else to do the grunt work?

- Love of money destroyed our family.

- To get a return on your money, you have to be willing to take a risk.

- Welfare is shameful.

- Good health is true wealth.

Catchy Phrases

Money messages come in many forms, some obvious, some covert. You may have heard catchy phrases, such as those on the facing page, that stick in your mind. Or you may have received nonverbal messages, which may take longer to identify but are just as powerful.

Money messages come from many sources, not just from people you know but also from your culture: books, movies, art, plays, music, advertising or political slogans, and other oft-used phrases.

Take a few minutes now to respond to the following six questions about money messages that have influenced your life. For each, write down as many messages as you can remember. Don't ponder each one too long; just start to write. One message will trigger the next until you come to a resting spot. If you cannot remember any messages, note that and go on. More messages may rise up in your consciousness as the days go by. Just keep adding them to your list.

Jotting down these words may sound silly or simple at first, but repeated phrases create ingrained expectations that can have a vise-like grip on the mind, and this is a great way to understand their hold.

1. **What messages about money did you receive from you mother?**

2. **What messages did you receive from your father?**

3. **Your grandparents?**

4. **Your friends?**

5. Your religious training?

6. Your teachers?

Putting Things into Context

Understanding not only your family role models, but also how the family models affect your current financial life, is the cornerstone of putting your spiritual values into financial practice. It is important to keep writing down your responses. The act of writing what you are aware of will keep the process in motion.

These next six questions focus on where you are today, financially and spiritually.

1. **Who handles the money in your present life?** Who makes the major financial decisions?

2. **How are money decisions or problems handled in your home today?** Is money discussed openly? Who is a part of the discussion?

3. **Describe how major financial decisions are made in your present household.**

4. **Is the money available in your household scarce or abundant?**

5. What feelings surface for you as you think of your current money situation?

6. What similarities do you see between your past and your present attitudes or behavior around money?

Decisions, Decisions

Climb up my apple tree

Shout down my rain barrel

Slide down my cellar door

And we'll be jolly friends forever more.

My mother always used to sing this little song to me. Many years later when I was married and had a family, my husband and I were searching for a new house. One of the houses we saw listed had both an apple tree and a cellar door. I loved it and we bought it, even though it wasn't the best financial deal for us. I was so happy to be in the house that I had often imagined from my mother's song and to think that I could pass on the joy of "an apple tree and a cellar door" to my kids. It wasn't until many years later that I understood the financial connection. A simple example, it showed me clearly that even the biggest economic decision, such as buying a house, is influenced by messages from childhood that have little to do with current financial calculations.

Money messages seem to surface most often when you have a big decision to make.

In fact, money messages seem to surface most often when we have a big decision to make. They may come to the fore as a sense of elation or certainty that causes us to rush to a decision. Or they may come to the fore as admonitions, warnings, or criticisms. Sometimes the message itself is unclear, but we have an uneasy feeling or a sense of doubt that keeps us from taking action.

Think of major financial decisions you have made, recently or in the past. Make a list below of your decisions and any money messages that may have influenced how you made it.

Decision	Money Message

What Matters to You?

By uncovering money messages, you are getting to your core attitudes and values—the very roots of your belief system. This process brings you face to face with some fundamental questions: Do you want to keep the myth you have had since childhood? Or do you want to create new messages that are more compatible with your life now?

Early messages have a lot of power. It is hard to question the value system you were raised in, or to disagree with it. Even if you question these beliefs only in your mind, you will feel the power of the pattern. Breaking the rules or stepping outside the code of behavior with which you were raised can be paralyzing. Often, keeping the rules is the only way to remain a part of the tribe, family, community, or religion. Break the rules, and you're out.

I witnessed this firsthand as a child. My mother, an Irish Catholic, married a German Jewish man. She defied the system—ethnic, religious, and familial—and was held accountable. She could no longer participate in the rituals of her own church because she had defied its rule not to marry outside the faith. Exclusion is a powerful lesson.

As an inquiring woman, you are questioning and coming to terms with your history, your financial life, and your spiritual life. In some cases, that may mean changing a particular message, or removing it from your mind.

Remember my friend with all the books? She laughed about being surrounded by books, but acknowledging the situation allowed her to identify and evaluate the money message she had inherited: that books could be her only luxury. Once she became aware of the power of her father's message, she was able to move beyond his rules about what was acceptable to buy for enjoyment.

In my case, the change was not so lighthearted. The severity of my financial situation required me to make major changes, and quickly. I was a divorced mother of five children without any support other than my salary. I had always carried a deeply embedded message: "Do not talk about your finances outside the household," but that message had to go. It was a survival issue. At the doctor's office, the orthodontist, the lawyer's office, the financial aid offices of the colleges my children attended—at all these places I had to loudly, clearly, and truthfully talk about the reality of my finances.

I was being pushed and prodded, for the sake of providing for myself and my children, to see the message to keep silent about money as useless for my present time and place. My mother's admonition that finances were a "family matter" acted as bondage, holding me to the myth. It was time for a new message.

Change is what can happen when you hold your money messages up to the light. But not every money message must go. Your task is to listen to each message that you have identified, understand its history, and evaluate its current use. Do you want to keep it? Use it? Change it? Get rid of it? These next three questions will help you consider which money messages still have value for you and which no longer work.

1. Which money messages that you grew up with are still true for you today? How do they influence you?

Message	Influence

2. Which money messages are not helpful to you now? Why?

Unhelpful Message	Why

3. Which money messages have value for you now? What is that value?

Valuable Message	Value

Recap

In the work you've done in this first chapter, I hope some new insights have come to you about the influences your *Money Messages* have on your current attitudes toward money. Understanding these habitual ways of thinking can open the windows of your mind to new understandings and possible beliefs.

With this awareness comes the opportunity to develop a new money mythology based on your own values, the opportunity to develop a personal response to your financial life. This is the true meaning of financial "response-ability."

As you continue on your money journey, I invite you to thoughtfully and meditatively respond to your own situation—with honesty, creativity, and a sense of purpose.

Chapter Two

Your Money Autobiography

What Is Your History?

*I*t is only when we "unpack" our emotional history that we can become aware of any patterned responses, unconscious motivations, and habitual behaviors. That is why I believe the second stage of The Money Journey Circle, writing *Your Money Autobiography*, is so important. There is research and scientific evidence supporting the fact that our bodies carry our emotional history in cellular memory as well as in mental memory. The ideas we hold become the operating system under which we live, move, and have our being. I believe this system of ideas has a presence as strong as our DNA, but instead of genetic material, it is made up of our family philosophy, cultural ethos, and spiritual beliefs.

Telling the story of your experiences and relationships with money has the potential to reveal many secrets about how you have related—and are still relating—to money in your life.

You will need to set aside time to write your money autobiography. Some people resist this, or find it hard to begin. However, there is a freedom that comes from writing a money autobiography that makes it well worth your time and effort.

Since money messages are not always apparent to the conscious mind, sometimes they will unfold only by questioning or in conversation. You may find it helpful

"Learning to think objectively about money is the key to making yourself free."

—Eliot Janeway, *economist*

to prepare your money autobiography with a group, or at least one other person, since your story or myth was developed in the group that was your family and community. Having a group to work with may help you examine your story more honestly. In solitude we are more prone to rationalize, deny, embellish, or otherwise temper the truth. In a group we are more able to gain insights and see emerging patterns as we share our stories.

An alternative to having others actively listen to you is to listen to yourself. You can speak out loud. And you can challenge yourself: "Is this really what happened? Have I conveniently 'forgotten' some key elements?"

However you approach it, the process of writing your own story will provide you with historical perspective on how your current relationship with money developed. This is your own personal money mythology.

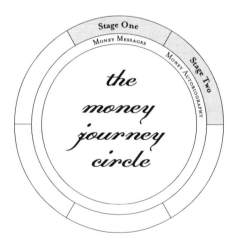

Starting Your Money Autobiography

The next few pages present a series of money autobiography questions that will help you recall your experiences and remember the feelings associated with each event. The questions are designed to help you think about any and all of the conditions that influenced your perception of the world and of the role of money in your life.

On the next page, answer each of the questions one at a time in narrative form, even by writing down just a phrase or a few words. Describe the scenes, experiences, and feelings that come to mind. Remember, this is your money story. It is not about how well you write, but about calling up memories on your path to making a deeper connection to your money. There is no right or wrong way to do this; simply note the experiences and feelings that come to mind.

"A light went on inside me when I realized how much my values of money came from my parents and how I try to force those values on my grown children."

—A WORKSHOP PARTICIPANT

29

1. **Start by describing the time in which you were born.** What were the economic conditions of the country while you were growing up? Was it wartime or peacetime? Prosperity or depression?

2. **Next, describe your family configuration.** Two parents? A single parent? Adoptive parents? Foster parents? Other siblings? Presence of grandparents?

3. **Describe your first home as best you can remember, noting how early the memory is.** Did you live in a house or apartment? Was it large or small? In a town, city, farm, or in another country? Did you have your own room, or did you share a room? How did this change over the years?

4. What are your early memories of family holidays? Vacations? Shopping trips?

5. Make note of any role models you had, real or fictional. What did they represent to you?

6. **What are your memories of high school?** Of clothes, cars, friends, parties, dates, sports, grades? What were the fashions, books, movies, ads, or trends of this time?

7. **What about higher education?** Did you go to college? Graduate school? Was money provided for your education? Did you receive scholarship funds? Did you work to pay tuition? How did you feel about money during those years?

8. Describe your first job and how much you earned. What was your experience of opening your first bank account, making your first investment, buying your first car, renting your first apartment, buying your first house, etc.?

9. **Describe whichever of the following are applicable: how you advanced in your career, grew your business, married, started a family, raised children, etc.**

10. **How has your gender affected your relationship with money?**

11. How has the amount of money you have had at different times in your life related to your feelings of self-worth?

12. **What are your memories of spiritual experiences in your community** (rituals, sacraments, celebrations, weddings, funerals, births, spiritual rites of passage, holidays, etc.)? Make note of any special words you remember hearing that relate money to these events.

13. **If you make contributions to religious or spiritual institutions or give to social and charitable causes, describe what influences your donations.**

14. Do you have memories of any significant spiritual experiences or conversations with others about spiritual experiences?

15. **Describe your relationship to spirituality**: Has spirituality been a core part of your daily life? Has it been confined to set times and services? Or is spirituality not even a part of your life?

Unpacking your history this way helps you to identify patterns and answer questions like "Why am I doing this now?" You see how your own story often repeats your family experience. In my workshops and book groups, women often come to an "aha" moment when they see how their actions the day before were nearly identical to their actions ten years ago. As I've noted before, it is helpful to do this work in a group or with at least one other woman. Sharing out loud enables images to emerge and invites feedback from others that can bring new awareness. If you are doing this work alone, review your answers, develop your story based on the flow of your life, and look for patterns that seem to persist through the years.

Creating a Money History Time Line

By answering these autobiographical questions, you have captured on paper an image of the circumstances of the life you were born into, and the information you assimilated about money throughout your life. Given the amount of information you have already recorded, you may be beginning to get a clearer perspective on your money myths and how they fit with your personal economic situation—and that of the larger world at different times in your life. Now take this one step further and plot your responses into a money history time line. This is a valuable tool that can help you break a lot of information down into manageable chunks.

On the time line that appears in the following pages, write in the years for each decade of your life. (If you feel you would like more space to write, simply use a blank sheet of paper or your journal.) Above the line, write any pleasant or satisfying experiences you had related to money during each decade of your life. Below the line, write any unpleasant or unsatisfying experiences you went through. Use your answers to the money autobiography questions as inspiration.

An Example of a Money History Time Line

Year 1940	Year 1950	Year 1960
Age 5	Age 10	Age 20

Pleasant, satisfying experiences

Selling lemonade	10 Given allowance	Inherited money
	15 Bought portable radio (first big purchase)	24 Good job and saved money
	17 First after-school job	

Unpleasant, unsatisfying experiences

Day 2, no one came but mother	Allowance tied to chores	Mother died and left me money and I didn't know what to do with it
	15 Bike stolen	25 Married to a controlling husband who didn't want competition earning money
		Stopped working

An Example of a Money History Time Line

Year 1970	Year 1980	Year 1990
Age 30	Age 40	Age 50

Pleasant, satisfying experiences

31 Bought house with money from inheritance	42 Remarried. Two incomes!	Remortgaged house and paid off all credit debt
33 Got a new job		

Unpleasant, unsatisfying experiences

	Divorced. Money dwindled after marriage to husband who was not responsible with money	Husband laid off
	Accumulated credit card debt	

Money History Time Line

Year ____   Year ____   Year ____

_____

Age 5   Age 10   Age 20

Pleasant, satisfying experiences

Unpleasant, unsatisfying experiences

Money History Time Line

Year ____   Year ____   Year ____

_____

Age 30   Age 40   Age 50

Pleasant, satisfying experiences

Unpleasant, unsatisfying experiences

Money History Time Line

Year ____   Year ____   Year ____

Age 60   Age 70   Age 80

Pleasant, satisfying experiences

Unpleasant, unsatisfying experiences

Sacred Space

Exploring your life experiences as they connect to money, perhaps for the first time, may bring up a lot of emotions. You may need to cry, laugh, or feel the pain of loss, missed opportunities, and beautiful moments that won't happen again in just that same form. In order to integrate all these feelings, I recommend the practice of meditation and the creation of sacred space. I like to call any place where you can sit, lie down, or walk in privacy a "sacred space." We have to live in a space of action and intensity, but it is in the sacred space that we find the calm and unity that lets us walk gracefully through life being exactly who we are.

There are many different forms of meditation, but all generally involve some kind of quiet release from thought. It is through integration that you will be able to bring your life history, your present moment, your spirituality, and your finances into a whole that is truly expressive of who you are. In the bustle and activity of daily life this is much harder to do. I have been practicing meditation with Marilyn Clements, a teacher in Stamford, Connecticut, and now I meditate daily. I feel the benefits flow into every corner of my life. If this is not something you are currently doing, you may want to consider beginning the practice. There are many teachers and many methods. One resource to begin your own search for a way to meditate is a book called *How to Meditate,* by Lawrence LeShan.

Think for a moment about how you might create a place of meditation and retreat for yourself. By that I mean a place where you can rest and accept the person you are and the gifts you have been given, a quiet place of reflection where you can be surrounded by objects you love. Here you can look over your life with respectful attention, review the new awareness you have come to observe, and prepare to move on.

If one way of creating a sacred space does not work out for you, another one will. This is so important to the process of leading an intentional life. Determine to sequester yourself, even for a few minutes at a time right in your own home, at planned intervals. It will benefit you and those who know you.

What sacred space looks like is somewhat different for everyone. A friend of mine creates her sacred space by putting on soft music—flute or harp—as soon as she wakes up. She lights a candle in her bedroom to remind her of the light of the divine. Then she goes about getting dressed.

However you create sacred space for yourself, it will help you develop resiliency. Having this quiet place in your home—and in your mind—grounds you so that you can handle the surprises that have the potential to throw you off kilter. Don't struggle to make your space mimic someone else's idea. Make it your own, whatever that looks or feels like for you.

Write a promise to yourself to create a sacred space. Be specific about how, when, and where you will set aside your space. Write this commitment on a card or piece of paper and put it where you will see it. This will give you an added incentive to carry it out. For example:

I will create a sacred space for myself in (name the room). It will have (candles, music, books, and a comfortable chair). I will spend (_minutes or _hours) in it every (_day, _week).

Recap

I wish I could see you to give you a warm smile, a gentle pat on the back, a few words of encouragement. You have accomplished much already. Your first two stages of the Money Journey are nearly complete: you have explored your own *Money Messages* and your unique *Money Autobiography*. Take a moment to reflect on the words of Eliot Janeway from the opening of this chapter: "Learning to think objectively about money is the key to making yourself free."

This is the message I hope you are beginning to experience. The work you are doing now is about freedom—the freedom to make decisions about what you really want without being restrained by ignorance, by other people's beliefs, or by the temptation to yield control over the money in your life.

There are many tracks that lead to bringing your financial life into spiritual perspective. And there will be moments on this journey when the process may seem like two steps forward and one step back. But be assured of this: you have made the most difficult decision of all—the decision to begin.

Ending Prayer

In my reading of the twentieth-century theologian Pierre Teilhard de Chardin, author of *The Divine Milieu*, I am inspired to think of our lives as having two threads: an inner thread and an outer thread. The inner thread contains all the ideas, attitudes, and knowledge of our life to date. The outer thread is composed of the circumstances we find ourselves in at any given moment. I invite you to use the following prayer, which I wrote in response to Teilhard de Chardin, as you continue to seek understanding and perspective on the role of money in your life:

> Give me the persistence to find the inner and outer threads of my life. Help me to have the courage to hold these threads up to the light, so that I can see the whole tapestry that is me, in body and soul. Lead me to see both the strengths and weaknesses of the weavings of my life. Encourage me to bind the threads together with love, so that doubled, they may work doubly hard for my good and the good of the world.

Chapter Three

Uncovering Your Money Facts and Feelings

Count Your Blessings

*I*n this chapter I will be asking you to identify specifics about your financial resources. But before you start to "count the money," I want you to "count your blessings." Annick, a friend of mine who follows the Islamic tradition of Sufi mysticism, tells me that she counts her money among her blessings. As a matter of fact, she sees money as a blessing and uses it intentionally so that the blessing she has received is passed along as she spends it. Your own blessings might include your health, intellectual capacity, family, friends, spiritual connections, community, and even the small "riches" you have—such as the unique clock you picked up in a European flea market when you were a college student traveling on five dollars a day; a series of photos of your family and friends; or a pair of ratty old slippers that soothe your tired feet at the end of the day better than any fancy shoes. These are your blessings as much as money is. In our consumerist society, we are often convinced that the only thing that counts is money that we can buy more things with.

Take note, too, of the intangible riches: the knowledge that your best friend would be at your side to share your joys or your sorrows; that your community would

the
money
journey
circle

"The challenge of mindfulness is to work with the very circumstances that you find yourself in."
—Jon Kabat-Zinn,
Full Catastrophe Living

55

help you in any emergency; that you can trust yourself and your intuition to take you to the next best step for yourself.

Does your real abundance come from laughter with the positive people in your life? A partner who listens to you? Children who are bringing your good counsel to reality in the daily story of their lives? Think, too, of important lessons—even good things—that have come out of difficult challenges you have faced, and of their value to you at this time in your life.

In cultures like that of the United States, where money has such a high priority, we can easily lose sight of its true value. Money is not the soul of existence, and we need to put our financial lives in perspective. This is not to deny the reality that money has its uses. One memory that comes to my mind when I do this next exercise is a shopping trip with an African friend. She spent her entire bonus on gifts for her family and friends. At first, I was concerned that she was spending so much. Then she put my thoughts to rest. "Money is nothing," she said. "Life is all about relationships. It makes me happy to buy these gifts, and everyone will be happy that I remembered them." At the top of my lists of abundances I, too, put my connections to other people. What is at the top of your list?

Describe all the wealth and abundance in your life that does not have a dollar sign attached to it.

What Do You Know?

I have come to believe that the beginning of transformation lies in identifying what you already know and what you do not yet know. Many of us simply do not know the facts of our financial life. We might even prefer it that way. Or, in the words of a woman who participated in one of my workshops, "I like to keep my numbers fuzzy because then I do not have to take responsibility for them."

"I know all the facts of my financial life. They fence me in. I see the immediate facts clearly but I cannot see beyond them. I feel limited by what I see. I feel I have no room for imagination or new decisions."

—A WORKSHOP PARTICIPANT

In my own life, there were many times when I could not bring myself to look directly at the facts of my financial life. Or I would look at some things, but not others. One of my favorite approaches to difficult money issues was to play Scarlett O'Hara, the heroine of *Gone with the Wind*, and repeat after her: "I'll think about that tomorrow."

I would find myself picking and choosing facts. I'd rationalize away anything that I didn't know or couldn't take care of. I'd tell myself that I was being responsible just because I took care of one easy thing, like paying a bill, and left the rest undone.

For many years, I would not look at the whole picture all at once. It was just too big for me. And I knew that once I understood the situation, I would have to make some decisions. I would have to accept the responsibility of becoming the primary decision maker in my family's financial affairs.

For many years I would not look at my financial picture . . . I knew that once I understood the situation, I would have to make some decisions.

Now I realize I was afraid of making decisions because I was afraid I would do the wrong thing. I also now realize that I did not know how to go about making an informed decision.

On the pages that follow, I am going to ask you to take an honest look at your financial facts—and then to move beyond these facts, to know the details but not get stuck on them. This *Facts and Feelings* stage of The Money Journey Circle starts with some fundamental questions, such as: Do you know where your financial records are? If you can't find something, do you know where you can look? If you have questions, do you know someone you could call for help?

But uncovering the necessary data is only half the picture. It is equally important to discover and connect with your emotional response to these facts. If you will take this section slowly, one segment at a time, I can help you do that.

Meditation for This Stage in Your Journey

I ask the universe for the wisdom and the courage to open my hands, my head, and my heart to the facts and figures of my financial life. My intention is to open my spirit to the transformation and freedom that the knowledge of those details can bring. I want to prepare my soul for using money wisely in ways that can truly enrich me and those who are near to me, as well as those who are far away, whom I may not even know, and whose needs I may not understand.

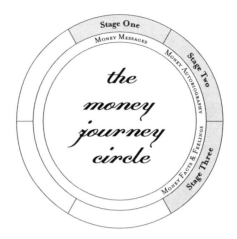

Financial Awareness Checklist

I am going to start you on your exploration with the following Financial Awareness Checklist. The goal is to help you identify what you know and where you need to find out more. This is not the time to worry or feel guilty; you are simply gathering useful information.

Do You . . .	**Yes**	**No**
Have a checking account or credit cards in your own name? (For example, if you are married, is it under Jane Doe, not Mrs. John Doe?)	___	___
Know how many credit cards you have?	___	___
Have a banker?	___	___
Know your banker?	___	___
Have a broker?	___	___
Know your broker?	___	___
Have an attorney?	___	___

	Yes	No
Know your attorney?	___	___
Have an accountant?	___	___
Know your accountant?	___	___
Know if you could borrow money in your own name?	___	___
Know what your credit report prepared by the major credit bureaus looks like?	___	___
Know how to order a copy of your credit report?	___	___
Make your own investment decisions?	___	___
Understand the tax return you sign?	___	___
Understand your retirement benefits?	___	___
Understand your spouse's retirement benefits and what rights you have to collect on them?	___	___
Have an Individual Retirement Account (IRA)?	___	___
Know how these benefits are invested?	___	___
Know your current insurance needs?	___	___

Know the specifics of your insurance coverage:

	Yes	No
Property?	___	___
Auto?	___	___
Health?	___	___
Disability?	___	___
Long-term care?	___	___

Have a current will? ___ ___

Put a check next to any of the following that you own in your own name:

___ Real Estate	___ CDs (Certificates of Deposit)
___ Mutual Funds	___ Valuable Personal Property
___ Treasury Bills	___ Bonds
___ Car	___ Savings Bonds
___ Stocks	___ Retirement Plan

Put a check next to any of the following terms that you could easily explain to a friend:

___ Net Worth	___ Treasury Bills
___ Stock	___ Mutual Fund
___ IRA	___ CD
___ 401-K	___ Stock Options
___ Cash Flow	___ Prime Rate
___ Bond	___ Compound Interest
___ Annuity	

Do you regularly do any of the following: **Yes**   **No**

Read financial books, magazines,
or the financial section of
a newspaper?   ___   ___

Listen to the financial news on
television?   ___   ___

	Yes	No
Visit web sites that contain financial information and instruction?	____	____
Talk to your friends about investments?	____	____
Consider how to share your resources with others?	____	____

Take a deep breath . . . you may have just crossed over into new territory. There is no need to be apprehensive. Remember that this is a time for awareness, not for pressure or guilt or fear. You can move along at your own pace. For now, take just a few more minutes to respond to these two reflective questions:

What gaps in your financial information do you need to fill in and where do you want to start?

How are you feeling right now as you start to get clearer about the breadth and depth of your understanding of basic financial facts?

Getting over the Hurdles

As I was in the middle of writing this chapter, I received the following e-mail from Candice Briggs of Battle Creek, Michigan, and I want to share it with you:

> As a self-employed counselor for over twenty-five years I am most interested in the emotional blocks that we place upon ourselves in relationship to money. As a Christian, I learned at a young age that "the love of money is wrong," and I have somehow twisted that to not allowing myself to experience money exchanges in a healthy way. Many women my age, in our fifties, turn to our spouses, who may not know the answers either, so we sit and "hope" and wait for something to rescue us from the "unknown" world of finance. It is my desire to understand finances more clearly and become more confident in my choices both spiritually and financially. It is time for me to face the fears that I have created around money and move ahead to help others.

Perhaps one of the biggest hurdles to get over in understanding your finances more clearly is to locate all of your data. Many women are tempted to stop here because they simply don't know where things are. One woman I know used to put important papers on top of the refrigerator. The problem was that she forgot what she put there and some of her papers fell to the floor behind the refrigerator. It wasn't until she moved from the house that she found those important papers. Be wary of certain nontraditional storage places!

Become a Collector

Being organized is a part of money management. There are several good books listed in the Resources section on how to get organized, and what blocks you from creating and maintaining order. For the moment, however, I want you to simply get a container that appeals to you—a cardboard box, a plastic storage unit, an unused suitcase—or to clear out a drawer. This container or drawer will become the temporary repository for your financial paperwork. You can organize your papers in a different form later, if you choose, but for now, just having the data collected in one place will aid you in moving forward.

Take your time. Even as you look for your records, you can continue to work on your money issues. You may be the kind of person who wants to spend three hours tracking down everything at once. Or you may prefer to take fifteen minutes a day until it is all gathered.

Remember to be attentive and open as you gather information. Inspiration and insights are close at hand. Think of creating order not as a chore, but as a spiritual task.

Here is a list of the records you will need to collect. As you find each one and put it in your special container, check it off the list. Remind yourself that this space is holding the tools you need to move forward on your spiritual money journey.

Financial Document Checklist

___ Checkbook

___ Savings Account Book

___ Bank Statements

___ Checking Account

___ Savings Account

___ CD Account

___ Money Market Account

___ Payroll Stubs for One Month

___ Insurance Policies

___ Life Insurance

___ Health Insurance

___ Disability Insurance

___ Homeowner's or Renter's Insurance

___ Auto Insurance

___ Long-term Care

___ Brokerage Statements

___ Bonds

___ Stocks

___ Mutual Funds

___ Annuities

___ Stock Certificates or Bonds

___ Car Title(s)

___ Property Deeds

___ List of Contents of Your Safe Deposit Box

___ Safe Deposit Keys

___ Records of All Retirement Funds

___ Copy of Your Will

___ Copy of Power of Attorney

___ Copy of Health Care Proxy

___ Medical Records

___ Deed to Cemetery Plot

___ Loan Statements

___ Home Mortgage Loan Balance

___ Auto Loan Balance

___ Student Loan Balance

___ Other Loan Balances

___ Most Recent Credit Card Statements

_____

_____

_____

_____

_____

___ Copy of Your Credit History

___ Other: _____

___ Other: _____

In the Dark No More

If there is no pressing, specific reason for looking at financial details, most people—women *and* men—do not have financial information readily available. Women in particular "are not socialized and educated to take control of their financial destiny," as Lisa Marsh Ryerson, president of Wells College, has observed. Even now, although many financial-management books have been written and courses have been given, many women feel that learning about or managing money is not what they are meant to do.

The good news is that women have the tools to connect to their financial lives. If you have been up in the air about at least some of your financial matters until now, collecting your key financial records will help you get grounded. A good place to start is to record the important names, addresses, phone numbers, and account numbers related to your finances. Compiling this information will not only save you time when you need to access your money, but more importantly, it will remind you that you are in charge. Knowing the very basic details, such as where you stash your bank statements or savings account records, will help you grow in your understanding of how you treat your financial life. And it is only as you understand your finances that you will be able to bring them into alignment with your spiritual values.

The next few pages provide some space for you to record the names and contact information for key financial people and institutions in your life. You can use this book as your record keeping system, or simply use these pages as a model for creating a system on a computer or in a notebook. Many people prefer to learn to use one of the computerized systems. Ask your friends, accountant, financial advisor, or computer specialist about which programs they recommend. Check for continuing education courses in your area to see if there are training courses on how to set up and use personal financial software programs. It could take just a couple of sessions to become comfortable with managing your finances electronically.

1. Key People

Attorney
Name _____
Address _____
Phone _____ Fax _____
E-mail _____ Web site _____

Accountant
Name _____
Address _____
Phone _____ Fax _____
E-mail _____ Web site _____

Banker

Name _____

Address _____

Phone _____ Fax _____

E-mail _____ Web site _____

Broker

Name _____

Address _____

Phone _____ Fax _____

E-mail _____ Web site _____

Financial Planner

Name _____

Address _____

Phone _____ Fax _____

E-mail _____ Web site _____

Insurance Agent

Name _____

Address _____

Phone _____ Fax _____

E-mail _____ Web site _____

Person Holding Power of Attorney

Name _____

Address _____

Phone _____ Fax _____

E-mail _____

Person Holding Health Care Proxy

Name _____

Address _____

Phone _____ Fax _____

E-mail _____

Tax Preparer

Name _____

Address _____

Phone _____ Fax _____

E-mail _____ Web site _____

2. Financial Institutions

Bank Account: Checking 1

Institution _____

Account # _____

Address _____

Phone _____ Fax _____

E-mail _____ Web site _____

Bank Account: Checking 2

Institution _____

Account # _____

Address _____

Phone _____ Fax _____

E-mail _____ Web site _____

Bank Account: Savings

Institution _____

Account # _____

Address _____

Phone _____ Fax _____

E-mail _____ Web site _____

Brokerage Account

Institution _____

Account # _____

Address _____

Phone _____ Fax _____

E-mail _____ Web site _____

Mutual Funds Account

Institution _____

Account # _____

Address _____

Phone _____ Fax _____

E-mail _____ Web site _____

IRA Account

Institution _____

Account # _____

Address _____

Phone _____ Fax _____

E-mail _____ Web site _____

3. Insurance Policies

Life

Company _____

Phone _____ Fax _____

Type _____ Amount _____

Insured _____

Policy # _____

Policy Owner _____

Beneficiary _____

E-mail _____ Web site _____

Health and Hospitalization

Company _____

Phone _____ Fax _____

Type _____ Amount _____

Policy # _____

Insured _____

E-mail _____ Web site _____

Disability

Company_____

Phone _____ Fax _____

Type _____ Amount _____

Policy # _____

Insured _____

E-mail _____ Web site _____

Automobile

Company_____

Phone _____ Fax _____

Type _____ Amount _____

Policy # _____

Insured _____

E-mail _____ Web site _____

Homeowner's/Renter's

Company_____

Phone _____ Fax _____

Type _____ Amount _____

Policy # _____

Insured _____

E-mail _____ Web site _____

Liability

Company_____

Phone _____ Fax _____

Type _____ Amount _____

Policy # _____

Insured _____

E-mail _____ Web site _____

Other

Company_____

Phone _____ Fax _____

Type _____ Amount _____

Policy # _____

Insured _____

E-mail _____ Web site _____

Other

Company_____

Phone _____ Fax _____

Type _____ Amount _____

Policy # _____

Insured _____

E-mail _____ Web site _____

Add other important accounts, names, and numbers that you want to include.

Take Heart

This is the point at which some women become overwhelmed by just looking at the information that is needed. I like to think of the process of collecting financial data as similar to collecting antiques or putting a puzzle together. When you first find an antique chair, for instance, you need to assess how much it's worth, take a look at any damage that has occurred over time, and then begin the loving work of restoring the chair to usefulness. When you complete a puzzle you have the delight of seeing the whole picture.

If you are uncovering the details of your financial facts for the first time, please be patient with yourself. Move through this chapter slowly. If there are pieces of information missing or if you have found some disturbing information, just let this observation be a part of the overall picture you are developing relative to your financial life. As you begin to understand the information you have gathered and to process your emotions regarding the data, you will be better able to make informed decisions and take the right action. Do not force solutions yet. Keep working through the book. Each step in the process is important.

Take heart from the following story of Jan Luckingham Fable, a psychotherapist who tells in her own words how she changed her approach to money:

> My family of origin was not a wealthy one, but when I was twelve years old, I learned I could sign my name on a store receipt and charge things at a department store. My father thought this was cute. He told me with a smile that I reminded him of his mother. He told me stories about how his mother would impulsively buy a dress or a hat and charge it. And then, later, when my grandfather had a fit about the bill, how she'd deny having bought anything—telling him the store had made a mistake. Next day she'd return the offending item and tell my

grandfather the store had corrected the error. The message to me was clear. My paternal grandmother was impulsive and irresponsible about money, and so was I—but it was okay because it made my father smile.

I continued to be impulsive and irresponsible with money for many, many years. I never reconciled a bank statement—in fact, I didn't even open them—until I was well into my forties. And until fairly recently, I continued to rely, without questions, on others, "on the experts," to invest for me, despite the fact that not asking questions in the past had led to a very large loss of money for me.

It's been a long journey from the piles of unopened bank statements and the joy of charging whenever and whatever I wanted. Now, I am self-employed, a homeowner, and diligent about paying credit card balances each month and saving for big purchases and needed home improvements. I've also begun to take an active interest in retirement investing, and I now ask questions of the experts whenever I don't understand. Even though that twelve-year-old girl still lives on in my heart of hearts, and there are days she still buys on impulse—and, occasionally, when money's tight, she feels scared and longs for some man to take care of her so she doesn't have to be the responsible one—the result has been that I've gained some small understanding of finance and a greater sense of financial purpose.

As a result of her own experience and her work as a therapist, Jan Fable now routinely asks her new clients specific questions about their past and present attitudes toward money, financial responsibility, and financial planning.

Focusing Your Attention

On the following pages, I am going to be asking you to begin filling in the blanks, identifying what you own and what you owe. I encourage you to make this experience as pleasant as possible. Put on your favorite music. Sit at a table that's been cleared for this purpose— except for, perhaps, a vase of flowers. Light a scented candle. Have a cup of tea or a cold drink beside you. Use colored pencils to write the information down. Relax. Focus your attention on identifying your precise financial circumstances. Remember, there is no time schedule here but yours. You can leave and come back to this process as often as you like.

As you work, you might want to place a written list of your goals where you can look at it often, to help yourself remember that this is truly something you want to do. Here's one example of such a list, which you may want to use or alter to encompass all of your goals around this issue:

My Goals for Understanding My Finances

- Be conscious about my financial resources.
- Integrate the spiritual aspects of my life with my financial picture.
- Look for the points where my financial life and my spiritual life intersect.

What Do You Own?

Liquid Assets (cash, or assets that can be exchanged for cash immediately)

Cash $_____
(cash on hand, checking and
savings accounts)

Money Market Funds   _____
(like a checking account with some
restrictions, usually pays interest)

CDs (Certificates of Deposit)   _____
(bank deposit with specified interest rate and
date of maturity; if you cash in ahead of time,
there is usually a penalty)

Life Insurance—Personal   _____
(cash value only)

TOTAL LIQUID ASSETS $_____

Near Liquid Assets (investments that can be sold for cash in a
few days)

Government Bonds/Corporate Bonds $_____
(investments that pay a fixed rate of return)

Municipal Bonds   _____
(fixed rate of return; not taxed)

Listed Stocks   _____
(stocks listed on the major stock exchanges;
gives you ownership in a company; daily value
of the stock is listed in the newspaper, on the
Internet, and on financial TV channels)

Mutual Funds   _____
(stocks or other investment vehicles bundled
into groups; shares are sold representing a
portion of the total value)

Other   _____

TOTAL NEAR LIQUID ASSETS $_____

Retirement Assets

Vested Pension $_____
(established by your employer; after a
specified time, or vesting term, you are
allowed to take it with you if you leave)

401-K Plans   _____
(retirement savings plan for corporate
employees)

403-B Plans   _____
(retirement savings plan for nonprofit
corporation employees)

IRAs (Individual Retirement Accounts)   _____
(retirement savings under your control,
established in a place of your choice)

SEP (Simplified Employee Pension) ⎯⎯⎯⎯
(essentially an IRA set up by your employer)

Keogh ⎯⎯⎯⎯
(retirement plan for self-employed individuals)

Annuities ⎯⎯⎯⎯
(an insurance investment vehicle purchased to
provide a stream of income at retirement)

Nonqualified Deferred Compensation ⎯⎯⎯⎯
(earnings not yet paid to you by your employer)

Other ⎯⎯⎯⎯

TOTAL RETIREMENT ASSETS $⎯⎯⎯⎯

Other Assets

Nonmarketable Stocks and Bonds $⎯⎯⎯⎯
(not readily salable and not registered on the
major exchanges)

Equity in Business ⎯⎯⎯⎯
(share of a business that you own)

Your Home ⎯⎯⎯⎯
(estimated current market value)

Seasonal Residence ⎯⎯⎯⎯
(summer house, ski house, other residence
you own and use)

Real Estate Investments ⎯⎯⎯⎯

Notes Receivable
(money owed to you that you can
reasonably expect to receive)

_____

Automobiles
(estimated current value)

_____

Household Items
(estimated value of furniture and fixtures
in your home if sold at a yard sale)

_____

Jewelry and Other Precious Items

_____

Collections
(antiques, books, whatever you collect that has
value individually and as a whole collection)

_____

Other

_____

TOTAL OTHER ASSETS

$_____

What Do You Owe?

Liabilities

Mortgage—Residential

$_____

Home Equity Line of Credit

_____

Mortgage on Other Properties

_____

Car Loan(s)

_____

Student Loan(s)

_____

Credit Card Debt _____

**Store Debt and Other Forms of
Debt Incurred by Use of "Plastic" Cards** _____

College Tuition _____

Other Notes Payable _____
(any type of note you've signed agreeing
to pay for something)

TOTAL LIABILITIES $_____

Putting It All Together

Total Assets

    Total Liquid Assets $_____
    (from page 77)

    Total Near Liquid Assets _____
    (from page 78)

    Total Retirement Assets _____
    (from page 79)

    Total Other Assets _____
    (from page 80)

TOTAL ASSETS $_____

LESS: TOTAL LIABILITIES $_____
(from this page)

NET WORTH $_____

What Are You Worth?

There, you've done it! You have collected the basic financial facts of your life.

Sometimes people confuse their self-worth with their net worth. If they have a lot of money, they feel great. If they don't, they belittle themselves. I once saw a cartoon that illustrates this point. It shows a group of well-dressed people sitting around a dinner table. The caption reads, "Money Is Life's Report Card." Although this seems to be a prevalent opinion, it is not necessarily true. Yet, for many people, their "net worth" implies "success" or "failure."

Think about these two terms: *net worth* and *self-worth*. Is your sense of self-worth affected by the details of your net worth? Note some of your thoughts here:

The question is not whether you have too much money, or too little to meet even your monthly expenses. While it is important to manage your money well if you have it, and to stay out of debt if you don't have enough, money is not the essence of your being. As a wonderful antidote to the "net worth equals self-worth" mentality, you might find Henri Nouwen's book *Life of the Beloved* helpful. Henri Nouwen tries to explain his belief in a spiritual life to a secular friend and begins by telling his friend that we are created out of love; he goes on to say, "You are not an accident, but a divine choice." Nouwen suggests taking time to ponder this thought and to let it permeate your being.

Connect with Your Feelings

As you have been working in this chapter to identify your financial facts, you have probably begun to identify your feelings about those facts. Your feelings about these important issues of life are where you and your spiritual beliefs come together, where you find your truth.

As you have been uncovering the financial facts of your life, you may have a stronger reaction to some items on your "assets and liabilities" lists than to others. For example, when you have money in your checking account, you feel good. When you are close to the cash reserve, you are frightened. Is one place closer to the spiritual core than another? Why should your checking account balance influence your feelings about yourself? What is the connection? The important thing is to acknowledge the feelings that arise as you work with your financial facts. The unexamined life can lead to paralysis, and unexplored feelings can inhibit action, even when you recognize in your mind the next steps that need to be taken.

Sometimes an emotional moment in the midst of documents and dollar signs can open doors.

Make a list of each type of account that seems to provoke a strong feeling in you. Write the dollar amount for each and a comment about your feelings. The following are samples of some comments I have heard women make:

Financial Fact	Feeling
IRA $ _____	Surprise: I have all this! Or . . . Fear: It's not enough.
Investment $ _____	Embarrassment: Don't know about it. Or . . . Frustration: Don't understand all this!
Credit card debt $ _____	Fear: How will I repay it? Or . . . Anger: How did this happen?

Remember, there is no "right" or "wrong" when it comes to feelings. Feelings are important clues about what lies at your core.

Financial Fact	Feeling

A Helping Hand

When I reflect on my early years of being a "grown-up"—a working woman, a wife, a mother, and then a single parent—I wish I had had a mentor or a friend who would have walked beside me on the journey into fiscal responsibility. As an only child, I embarked on a lonely learning process through many courses, conversations, and experiences. Perhaps you, too, are feeling lonely on this money journey.

Do you feel like you need more support? Or do you need people who are affected by your decisions to participate in this process with you? If so, write down the names of people you would like to have with you on this journey below. Then put their contact information next to the names.

Name   **Phone**   **E-mail**

You can include other people in your work in a variety of ways:

- Contact one of the people on your list and tell her (or him) that you are working on your financial facts. Explain why it is hard for you and ask this person simply to be available to listen, take a break with you, or celebrate each step with you when you complete it.

- Share with someone the joy that you are experiencing in beginning to take charge of your finances.

- Talk to a person who is central to the decisions you are making. Ask him or her for input.

- Invite others to create a group with you to share in the process of the spiritual money journey.

- Let others know about emotions that may be surfacing for you. Finances can often bring up emotions that you can't quite identify, and other people can offer support. Sometimes that happens just before a breakthrough or a new understanding.

Remember: At the precise moment you feel most vulnerable, you may be coming into your power. Once you know the story of your financial plusses and minuses, once you give yourself the authority to be in charge, there's no turning back to ignorance. You are giving yourself a gift and allowing yourself to replace negative messages with a sense of power and competence.

At the precise moment you feel most vulnerable, you may be coming into your power.

Call in the Experts

As you have collected your information, have you found holes? Perhaps you've never hired an accountant or an attorney before. Or maybe you haven't granted anyone a Power of Attorney or Health Care Proxy.

If someone in your life—husband, child, parent, friend—is taking care of your finances for you, you might feel that hiring financial help would be "betraying" that person. Ask yourself, "Is the person currently monitoring my finances doing such a good job that I don't even have to *peek* at what's going on?"

Or perhaps there is nobody in charge. I've heard some women say that if they take decisions about their money into their own hands, they have a sense of "falling from grace." Are you concerned that if you take charge, God or some unknown power will let go?

Here are some questions to consider:

◆ Can I manage my money myself?

◆ Can I let someone else do it entirely?

◆ Can I work in partnership with a professional or other knowledgeable, caring person?

If you think professional help may be a good idea for you, get recommendations from friends or a local professional society. Interview anyone you are considering. It is normal practice in these fields. You are not "wasting" someone's time. Professionals expect to spend some time discussing their approach, their credentials, and, of course, their fees. Here are some simple guidelines for getting financial help:

◆ Take your time. Do not make hasty decisions.

◆ Research your choices.

◆ Seek references and referrals for all professionals you consider hiring.

◆ Interview someone before engaging his or her services.

◆ Pay attention to your intuition. For example, you may have a gut instinct that alerts you to an unknown danger or a less than satisfactory situation. Note that feeling. Or in a quiet introspective moment you may have an inspired thought that seems to lead you in a new direction. Check it out.

◆ Be sure the professional you choose understands your values and will honor them in the work you do together.

I had to learn how to choose a professional by choosing the wrong one first. I paid his bill and moved on until I found a professional I liked and could work with well. Making mistakes is part of any learning process. Allow yourself room for this to happen and count it as part of the cost of your "financial education."

Recap

This chapter has focused on empowerment through knowledge of both your *Money Facts and Feelings*. It has also encouraged you to take charge of your financial life. You have done a lot of the work of organizing your finances, but at this moment you may not yet have a sense of accomplishment or a feeling of peace. You may still be experiencing an uneasiness, almost a foreboding, that comes with walking into the unknown—especially if you were previously unaware of your own or your family's total financial picture.

Continue to trust your intuition. Continue to describe your feelings. What matters is that you are intentionally seeking knowledge and clarifying your financial affairs.

Take a minute to note how you are feeling about being on this spiritual money journey. Do you feel any different than you did when you first decided to uncover your financial facts?

Chapter Four

Creating Alignment

Moving On

*Y*ou have come a long way! By doing the exercises with attention and intention, you have made some breakthroughs already and I want to stop here and encourage you to acknowledge them. I base my belief in your progress on the thousands of women I've met in workshops who reach this point and have an "aha!" moment. What are some of the steps you may have accomplished?

- ◆ Understanding what kind of money messages have been reaching your consciousness since you were born.

- ◆ Identifying some of your resistance to organizing your finances.

- ◆ Acquiring a measure of support by finding a partner or a group of women to share your work with.

- ◆ Compiling essential financial data.

- ◆ Establishing a special space to store your information.

- ◆ Recording your financial facts in a clear, readable format.

Don't be discouraged if you haven't accomplished all of this. Everyone moves at a individual pace of discovery. If you feel stuck, write down exactly where you're

the money journey circle

"There is guidance for each of us, and by lowly listening, we shall hear the right word."

—Ralph Waldo Emerson,
Spiritual Laws

stuck. Ask yourself, "Why am I stuck?" Then answer, "I am stuck here because … " Keep asking yourself this question until you can clearly articulate your answer. Sometimes the first thing that comes into your mind is the truest. At other times the answer eludes you for a while. For example, a woman called for investment advice. She was looking for a temporary investment for $200,000. I offered some choices and nothing seemed to be right for her. After many questions, she acknowledged that the $200,000 was an insurance payment on her mother's life insurance policy. She then started to cry and told me that she knew when she cashed that check it was the final step in acknowledging her mother's death. This insight surprised her, as she had thought she just couldn't make an investment decision.

Alignment doesn't nec- essarily show up as a glamorous moment, but as the coming together of intention and action.

The important thing is to work on your finances by holding this book in your hands and the intention in your heart. Wherever you find yourself on this path, you are on your way to a new financial awareness which will surely benefit you in ways you can't even imagine yet. The effort you make now is directed toward fulfilling a powerful purpose: to align your financial reality with a larger, spiritual reality—*who you are, what you care about, and how you want to live your life.*

At this specific stage of The Money Journey Circle you are at the point of seeking *Alignment*, the ability to integrate your facts, feelings, and actions with your spiritual core.

The Timing of Alignment

A few years ago, I led a workshop for a group of women entrepreneurs. Looking back on the experience, I can see now that I was in the middle of the "stream of power and wisdom," as Ralph Waldo Emerson so elegantly described it. But it surely didn't seem so at the time, since I was situated in a bland conference room in a nondescript office building on a chilly November afternoon.

Alignment is like that. It doesn't necessarily show up as a glamorous moment, but as the coming together of intention and action, wherever and whenever that happens. And when our alignment connects with the alignment of other people who are seeking purposes that intersect with ours, synchronicity happens!

One of the participants in that November workshop was a journalist named Joanne Kabak. She was there because she wanted to increase the income from her writing so that it would more fairly match her growing skills and reflect the economics of the current marketplace. She had returned to work to build a career as a journalist after stopping her work as a CPA to raise her children. Now that the kids were older, she wanted to make more of a financial contribution to her household, to help pay the mortgage and the daily expenses. What's more, she wanted to do so without compromising her intention to write about what was valuable and meaningful to her.

As you consciously bring your actions in line with your spirit, things happen.

My intention for that workshop was to help women "prosper" in every sense of the word. I wanted to help other women come to grips with their finances and move beyond their current monetary needs to their core desires and their spiritual "call." I came to encourage them to listen to and act on their inner voice, the one that tries to be heard above the din of the material world. At the same time, I still had my own unfulfilled dream: to write about my work, my beliefs, and my hopes for women's breakthrough in money matters. I needed a teacher in order to do that writing.

Enter the journalist, Joanne, who happened to be in my small group. As she expressed her desire to write, teach her craft, and earn money from her skills, her goals intersected with my intention to communicate my message with clarity. We entered the "stream of power and wisdom" together at that moment, starting a relationship that has taken us through many collaborations, including articles, workshop materials, brochures, and of course, this book.

The funny thing is, we had met a couple of times before, when Joanne was a journalist at a local newspaper and I was designing and conducting seminars on women and money for that paper. She even interviewed me and wrote about me. But our intentions were not in line at that time ... not until we met again at the right moment.

That's the way alignment often works. As you consciously bring your actions in line with your spirit, things happen without being forced, sometimes without being noticed until later. What starts to come through is the "lightness of being," the whisper of energy you sometimes feel after good exercise or an inspiring concert. You might not be able to put your finger on it, but you can surely feel yourself becoming lighter, gently blown as by a soft wind into a new place, project, or perspective.

Consider your timing for a moment. What is happening in your life at this juncture that made you decide to pick up this book? Why are you interested in looking at your finances at this particular time? The answers are part of the story of your alignment. Take a few moments to consider this question:

Why are you focusing on money and spirituality now? What drew you to this process at this time in your life?

The Flow of Money

The previous chapter focused on the state of your finances. Your list of assets and liabilities is a financial fact as of a certain date. It's like a snapshot of your financial life. In the next stage of your Money Journey, I am going to ask you to look at the flow of your finances, how money comes in and goes out. Cash flow is like a personal video of your financial life.

I believe understanding your cash flow is an essential ingredient in reaching alignment. It is like one of those levelers that carpenters use, a tool that tells you if your line is straight, if you are off the mark, or if you must make an adjustment.

A cash flow statement, prepared carefully, honestly, and with enough detail, can let you know whether or not your *cash in* is equal to your *cash out*. It informs you about the amount you may be over-spending, or the amount of discretionary income remaining after expenses. It provides you with the hard evidence you need to answer a critical question: "Am I spending my money wisely and well, the way I want to, or am I spending money habitually, on things I don't really care about?"

Why?

You might be asking, "Do I really need to do all the work of creating a cash flow statement? What do I need to know all those numbers for?" I can think of at least five reasons why it is helpful to prepare a cash flow:

- ◆ To clarify the sources of your money and the ways in which you spend it.

- ◆ To clarify your values.

- ◆ To reflect on your money flow and your values together.

- To begin the lifelong process of bringing your money and your spiritual life in line with each other.

- To create alignment, integration, and integrity in your life.

Convergence

I want to tell you about a woman I met named Sue Roselle at a book group. When she examined her spending, she saw that there were major cash outflows going to her hometown of Pittsburgh: six airfares in a year, big phone bills, contributions to her home church. She realized that even though her body—and her job—were in Chicago, her heart and soul were in Pittsburgh.

At the same time, she was feeling repeated disappointment about her job and her company. That discontent hit home one day when she felt she really needed someone to talk to about her job. She realized she didn't have anyone to call in Chicago. She had been so intent on her work that she had forgotten to make friends!

What good was a six-figure salary if it meant an eighty-hour week, and a lack of friends, family, social relationships? She took the time to ask herself, "What do I really want in life? What is important to me?"

The convergence of her money facts, her discontent, her attention to her soul's needs, and her connection to her family brought her into a place of alignment. She stopped sacrificing the personal for the professional and returned to Pittsburgh for the pleasures of having her family nearby and living a simpler lifestyle. She found a new job with people she respects—at half her previous salary—but now her eyes glow with a deep satisfaction when she smiles and talks about her life.

The very data of our lives can be a wake-up call if we pay attention to them and consider them in connection with how much we feel in alignment, how much our life makes sense to us. It is hard to feel that everything is going well if we are overspending. Similarly, what are the issues we have to face if we have enough money but we dread getting up in the morning?

Know the Flow

Your checkbook, credit cards, tax returns, bills, day planner, and computer files can provide the information of your daily financial life. They tell you where you've been, what you've done, how much it cost to be there, and what you've brought home. They tell you about the transactions you enter into, day by day.

"I notice that when my financial behavior connects with how I truly feel, I make decisions easily and I am not conflicted."

—A WORKSHOP PARTICIPANT

If you dig a little deeper, you will see the data also tell you what you enjoy, how you stay healthy, what is important to you. Your priorities are crystal clear in these records. Become comfortable looking at your bank statements and your bills, not just as items to check off, but as the story of your life. These records have become the twenty-first-century diaries.

To help you prepare your own cash flow statement, I have included two different cash flow forms to choose from. You can decide on the level of detail you want and work with the form that fits you best.

Version One: Detailed Cash Flow

To get a comprehensive overview, you can review your finances for one complete year on a twelve-month form. Enter the money you received and the money you spent in the appropriate months. For example, dividends are usually paid quarterly, so you would enter this income in the four appropriate months of the year. Salaries, on the other hand, may come in on a weekly or biweekly basis, and bonuses on an annual basis. Some expenditures are weekly (such as food), monthly (such as the mortgage or rent), quarterly (such as insurance bills), or annually (such as taxes). Entering your income or expenses in the month in which they occur will give you a more accurate financial picture.

Version Two: Summary Cash Flow

If, on the other hand, you are not concerned with this level of detail, you can prepare a more simplified cash flow. Estimate one month's income and expenses and then multiply this by twelve to get an average annual picture.

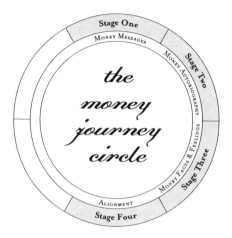

Getting Ready

Whichever form you choose, preparing a cash flow statement is an important step in bringing your financial and spiritual values into alignment. It may require some work, but it does not have to be unpleasant. Here are a few suggestions for making the process easier and more fun:

- ◆ You might want to copy the cash flow form you choose onto colored paper—sunny yellow or lavender are two of my favorites. Colors help many women overcome their aversion to working with black-and-white columns of numbers.

- ◆ Personalize the form. Are there items not listed on the form that you want to include, or items that you want to eliminate? This is *your* story, and it is different from anyone else's. I have identified only basic categories. You probably have other ones that are specific to your lifestyle. Add them to the form.

- ◆ You may want to use colored pens and pencils to record your numbers.

- ◆ You may also want to create a computer spreadsheet by using the popular program Excel or the personal financial management program Quicken.

- ◆ Choose a happy place to do the work. Play music. Be comfortable. Let the sunshine in.

- ◆ Plan a special time to do this. Otherwise you may keep putting it off. Plan something pleasing to do afterward, and think up rewards along the way.

Before you start, read the sidebar on "What My Cash Flow Can Tell Me" to help yourself remember why you are doing this work. You may want to bookmark this page and refer to it often to remind yourself of your greater goals in doing this work.

What My Cash Flow Can Tell Me

- How I take in money. When and how the money comes in.

- For what reasons, or under what circumstances, I release that money back out into the world (in other words, spend it).

- What my true necessities are.

- If I am living at, above, or below my income.

- What I really care about.

- Where my money flow and my values are in harmony.

- If I am using my money for what is important to me.

- What changes I could realistically make to align my financial and spiritual life.

The Ins and Outs of Money
Version One: Detailed Cash Flow

INCOME	Jan	Feb	Mar	April	May
Income 1 (before tax withholdings)	_____	_____	_____	_____	_____
Income 2 (before tax withholdings)	_____	_____	_____	_____	_____
Bonus	_____	_____	_____	_____	_____
Dividends					
From Stocks	_____	_____	_____	_____	_____
From Money Market Funds	_____	_____	_____	_____	_____
Interest					
From Treasury Bills and Notes or Other Government Issues	_____	_____	_____	_____	_____
From Saving Accounts	_____	_____	_____	_____	_____
From Other Sources (such as municipal bonds or personal loans)	_____	_____	_____	_____	_____
Additional Income					
From Pensions	_____	_____	_____	_____	_____
From Trust Funds	_____	_____	_____	_____	_____
From Rents/Real Estate	_____	_____	_____	_____	_____
Social Security Income	_____	_____	_____	_____	_____
Income from Partnerships or Other Business Investments	_____	_____	_____	_____	_____
Sales of Securities	_____	_____	_____	_____	_____
Other Income from Whatever Source	_____	_____	_____	_____	_____
TOTAL INCOME	_____	_____	_____	_____	_____

June	July	Aug	Sept	Oct	Nov	Dec	YEAR
————	————	————	————	————	————	————	————
————	————	————	————	————	————	————	————
————	————	————	————	————	————	————	————
————	————	————	————	————	————	————	————
————	————	————	————	————	————	————	————
————	————	————	————	————	————	————	————
————	————	————	————	————	————	————	————
————	————	————	————	————	————	————	————
————	————	————	————	————	————	————	————
————	————	————	————	————	————	————	————
————	————	————	————	————	————	————	————
————	————	————	————	————	————	————	————
————	————	————	————	————	————	————	————

Version One: Continued

NECESSARY EXPENDITURES	Jan	Feb	Mar	April	May
Mortgage/Rent					
Food/Groceries					
Utilities/Telephone					
Home Maintenance					
Clothing/Cleaning					
Personal Needs					
Transportation Expenses					
Medical/Dental					
Insurance Payments					
Medical					
Disability					
Life					
Car					
Personal Property					
Other					
Credit Card Payments					
Debt/Loan Payments					
Taxes					
Real Estate					
Personal Property or Other					
State/Local Tax					
Estimated Income Tax Payments					
Payroll Deductions/Tax Payments					
Federal/State					
Social Security					
Medicare					
Other					
TOTAL NECESSARY EXPENDITURES					

June	July	Aug	Sept	Oct	Nov	Dec	YEAR
____	____	____	____	____	____	____	____
____	____	____	____	____	____	____	____
____	____	____	____	____	____	____	____
____	____	____	____	____	____	____	____
____	____	____	____	____	____	____	____
____	____	____	____	____	____	____	____
____	____	____	____	____	____	____	____
____	____	____	____	____	____	____	____
____	____	____	____	____	____	____	____
____	____	____	____	____	____	____	____
____	____	____	____	____	____	____	____
____	____	____	____	____	____	____	____
____	____	____	____	____	____	____	____
____	____	____	____	____	____	____	____
____	____	____	____	____	____	____	____
____	____	____	____	____	____	____	____
____	____	____	____	____	____	____	____
____	____	____	____	____	____	____	____
____	____	____	____	____	____	____	____
____	____	____	____	____	____	____	____
____	____	____	____	____	____	____	____

Version One: Continued

DISCRETIONARY EXPENDITURES	Jan	Feb	Mar	April	May
Vacations/Travel					
Recreation					
Entertainment					
Dining Out					
Contributions					
Gifts					
Family Support					
Household Furnishings					
Home Improvements					
Pets					
Education Funding					
Savings					
Investments					
Other					
Other					
Other					
TOTAL DISCRETIONARY EXPENDITURES					

June	July	Aug	Sept	Oct	Nov	Dec	YEAR
————	————	————	————	————	————	————	————
————	————	————	————	————	————	————	————
————	————	————	————	————	————	————	————
————	————	————	————	————	————	————	————
————	————	————	————	————	————	————	————
————	————	————	————	————	————	————	————
————	————	————	————	————	————	————	————
————	————	————	————	————	————	————	————
————	————	————	————	————	————	————	————
————	————	————	————	————	————	————	————
————	————	————	————	————	————	————	————
————	————	————	————	————	————	————	————
————	————	————	————	————	————	————	————
————	————	————	————	————	————	————	————
————	————	————	————	————	————	————	————
————	————	————	————	————	————	————	————
————	————	————	————	————	————	————	————

My Summary: Version One

MY INCOME _____

MY NECESSARY EXPENDITURES (subtract) _____

MY DISCRETIONARY EXPENDITURES (subtract) _____

MY NET CASH FLOW _____

Version Two: Summary Cash Flow

INCOME	Average Month	YEAR
Income 1 (before tax withholdings)	_____	_____
Income 2 (before tax withholdings)	_____	_____
Bonus	_____	_____
Dividends		
From Stocks	_____	_____
From Money Market Funds	_____	_____
Interest		
From Treasury Bills and Notes or Other Government Issues	_____	_____
From Saving Accounts	_____	_____

From Other Sources
    (such as municipal bonds or
    personal loans)
	_____	_____

Additional Income		
From Pensions	_____	_____
From Trust Funds	_____	_____
From Rents/Real Estate	_____	_____
Social Security Income	_____	_____
Income from Partnerships **or Other Business Investments**	_____	_____
Sales of Securities	_____	_____
Other Income from Whatever Source	_____	_____
TOTAL INCOME	_____	_____

Version Two: Continued

NECESSARY EXPENDITURES	Average Month	YEAR
Mortgage/Rent	_____	_____
Food/Groceries	_____	_____
Utilities/Telephone	_____	_____
Home Maintenance	_____	_____
Clothing/Cleaning	_____	_____
Personal Needs	_____	_____
Transportation Expenses	_____	_____
Medical/Dental	_____	_____
Insurance Payments		
Medical	_____	_____
Disability	_____	_____
Life	_____	_____
Car	_____	_____
Personal Property	_____	_____
Other	_____	_____
Credit Card Payments	_____	_____
Debt/Loan Payments	_____	_____
Taxes		
Real Estate	_____	_____
Personal Property or Other State/Local Tax	_____	_____
Estimated Income Tax Payments	_____	
Payroll Deductions/Tax Payments		
Federal/State	_____	_____
Social Security	_____	_____
Medicare	_____	_____
Other	_____	_____
TOTAL NECESSARY EXPENDITURES	_____	_____

Version Two: Contintued

DISCRETIONARY EXPENDITURES	Average Month	YEAR
Vacations/Travel	_____	_____
Recreation	_____	_____
Entertainment	_____	_____
Dining Out	_____	_____
Contributions	_____	_____
Gifts	_____	_____
Family Support	_____	_____
Household Furnishings	_____	_____
Home Improvements	_____	_____
Pets	_____	_____
Education Funding	_____	_____
Savings	_____	_____
Investments	_____	_____
Other	_____	_____
Other	_____	_____
Other	_____	_____
TOTAL DISCRETIONARY EXPENDITURES	_____	_____

My Summary: Version Two

MY INCOME	_____
MY NECESSARY EXPENDITURES (subtract)	_____
MY DISCRETIONARY EXPENDITURES (subtract)	_____
MY NET CASH FLOW	_____

What Do the Numbers Tell You?

Now that you have done the work of preparing a cash flow statement, the next step is to figure out what all these numbers tell you. What can you learn from this numerical picture of your financial life?

One by one, quietly, thoughtfully consider the following six questions:

1. **How do you feel about the cash flow statement you have created?**

2. **Are there changes you need to make?** For example, are all your health care needs taken care of, or are you putting them off because you feel you don't have the money?

3. **Are there any changes you want to make?** For example, if

you are taking in more money than you need, would you like to give some away?

4. **What are some of the discretionary categories that take a measurable chunk of your money?**

5. **Are your earnings at a level that reflects the value of your**

work and your belief system?

6. **Do you see any spending that needs re-evaluating?**

A Balancing Act

In simple terms, alignment entails bringing different components into balance. This book is about learning to balance our financial needs and wants with our spiritual values and goals. Inherent in the very design of the human being is the yearning for alignment—the integration of desire, intention, action, and result.

This intertwining of all our experiences, feelings, and intellect with the external circumstances of our daily life is something close to a spiritual DNA, a God-essence that is in our very cells.

When we are in alignment, we are acting out of that God-essence. Think of alignment as an orchestra. If all the "players"—mind, body, and spirit—are in tune, the music is harmonious. But if one section is "off key," the whole orchestra sounds out of tune.

Your financial life is not a solo instrument. It is not separate and distinct from the orchestra of who you are.

What I am suggesting is that your financial life is not a solo instrument. It is not separate and distinct from the orchestra of who you are—although it may feel that way when you look only at balance sheets and checkbooks. How you use your money and resources is an integral part of your essence.

What's Important to You?

I am going to ask you to set aside your cash flow statement for a moment and take some time to focus on what is and isn't making you happy in your life.

Like Sue, the Chicago woman who moved to Pittsburgh, do you have times when you're working long hours and not having enough time for relationships? Do you ever find yourself thinking about living your life with less money but more satisfaction, and then the image leaves you and you go back to your tasks?

In my case, the images that I have from my travels to Haiti, Guatemala, Kenya, and Mexico cause me the greatest discontent. I know that many a child in those countries goes without an education—all for lack of about eighty dollars, which would pay for a year's worth of schooling. And then I find myself dropping forty dollars on flowers for my front doorstep.

Yet when I put the flowers out, my memory flashes back to a scene in Sarajevo. When I visited the city in 1996, I stood in the courtyard of an apartment complex that had survived serious bombing. Not all the buildings were intact, but each of those that were had balconies supporting window boxes with cascades of flowers. It created a visual smorgasbord of color—a nourishment for the eye and the heart. I felt the link between my peaceful home in the suburbs of the U.S. and this city torn up by mindless warfare. The contrast couldn't have been more extreme. In my own home, I want the same thing: the beauty and peace that lovely flowers can bring.

> *"I began to wonder: suppose I were hit by a Mack truck tomorrow; how would my check book stubs reflect what I cared about?"*
> —GLORIA STEINEM,
> *Moving beyond Words*

Sue experienced alignment when she moved back to Pittsburgh and rearranged her life. I experience alignment when I lead trips to Haiti or Kenya to initiate microlending projects. And I experience the same alignment when I recognize that I am spending money on flowers in order to acknowledge beauty and to bring a moment of joy to myself and my neighbors, who often remark what a pleasure it is to see the daffodils and pansies in bloom.

What is important to you? The following four questions will help you assess whether your use of money is in line with what you really care about.

1. **What do you want?** What do you care about for yourself, your family, your neighborhood or city, the global community? Don't be concerned about whether each item is a reality in your life. Simply ask yourself, "What am I really passionate about?"

2. **Now list some of your discontents.** What do you see that isn't working in your own life, or in the larger world? What would you want to change if you could?

3. **What part of your cash flow is in line with what you really care about?**

4. **What part of your cash flow seems to be in conflict with what you really care about?**

Recap

A friend of mine frequently reminds me of this piece of wisdom: "Pay attention to the details; God is in the details."

This chapter has certainly brought you face-to-face with the financial details of your life. I hope the cash-flow exercise has given you a deeper awareness of your economic habits and attitudes. If so, it has accomplished its task of calling your attention to the details that shape your financial life. The question I have asked you to consider is whether your financial life is in *Alignment* with your spiritual values, with what matters most to you.

Think about this statement for a moment: "Each detail, each financial decision, has the potential to bring my attention to other possible alternatives."

I believe this is true. Every time we make a financial decision, we have the potential to make a choice that is different from our habitual behavior. But I also believe that when we are out and about in our economic lives, it is too late to give serious consideration to the actions we want to take. We need to become aware and decide on our actions in the quiet of our deepest self, at the soul level.

Bring your heightened personal financial awareness to prayer level or an intentional level as you consider what is next for you on your Money Journey.

A Prayer for This Stage of Your Journey

Help me to see any changes I must make.

Help me find the courage to make the changes.

Help me to be peaceful even when I am uncomfortable.

Help me rejoice in the new feeling of alignment.

Chapter Five

Dream On

Seeing the Future

Many women today find their dreams are blocked by a seemingly insurmountable obstacle: *money*. Some aspect of not having money seems to stop the flow for them and they are paralyzed by a sense of scarcity. On the other hand, and this may surprise some of you, *having* money can also be a stumbling block! Some people I encounter express a sense of unworthiness or guilt at having too much. These conditions may seem like polar opposites, but they come from the same sources: ignorance of money, fear of money, lack of self-esteem, and a misunderstanding about the place, power, and purpose of money.

One of my goals in writing this book is to help you remove money as an obstacle to your dreams and turn it into a comfortable companion to your spirit. So far, you have looked at money in many different ways:

- Identifying your personal money messages.

- Recording your personal money mythology.

- Detailing the facts of your cash flow.

- Identifying your core values.

- Expressing what is important to you.

- Acknowledging how your financial and spiritual lives are or aren't aligned.

"If one advances confidently in the direction of [her] dreams and endeavors to live the life [she] has imaged, [she] will meet with a success unexpected in common hours."
—Henry David Thoreau, *Walden*

Now that you've done the work of the previous chapters, it is time to integrate your facts, feelings, and actions with your spiritual core. Another way to view this step is that it will link your finances with your inner desires and outer actions. This fifth stage of The Money Journey Circle focuses on *Dreams*. It is time to open yourself to the idea of "call," a word I use to describe the notion that your life has a purpose and that you seek to know what that purpose is; as you begin to intuit, hear, or understand that purpose, you take steps toward manifesting it in the outer world . This is the stage of seeing your future as an expression of your true self, not something

A Meditation for This Stage of Your Journey

Universal Spirit, open my mind to the possibility of call, the inner voice that whispers direction to me. Give me the ability to see, hear, feel, intuit, perceive, and know in some way the path that is open to me.

Enable me to overcome my blocks and my fears. Help me to understand that my resources—talents, money, and the blessings of family and friends—are part of the circle of love you provide for me.

Expand my vision to help me see that the difficulties and challenges of my life are my teachers. Enable me to receive them graciously.

Encourage me as I connect my financial resources to my spiritual resources. Shed a bright light so that the creative path of my life may become more obvious to me. Support me as the miracles of my life take shape.

imposed on you by others. You create your future by moving consciously toward an intentional life. What happens when you get those inklings of what you'd like to be doing? Don't disregard them. Consider them a sort of "divine whisper." What I'm asking you to do throughout this chapter is to pay attention to these inklings and to readjust your attitude toward money so that you have the practical will power to manifest the dreams and whispers of your soul.

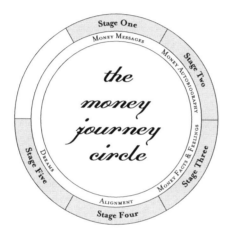

"But I Can't ..."

There are many different ways—a vision, a personal experience, a "funny" feeling—in which a new direction can become known to you, and there is often a common response: "But I can't do that. I don't have the money, the courage, the knowledge, the ability ... to start a new career, fund a program, learn a skill, sell my business, make a difference, I just don't deserve to do what I really want to do."

Marleen Salko, a friend of mine who was running a very successful yoga studio, had a yearning to have more time for herself, perhaps to travel and visit her family. She especially wanted to be relieved of the administrative details of running a business. For a few years she had been having desires and thoughts nudging her toward gaining more free time. The more she began to see these desires as valid, the more she increased her chances of acting on them.

Whatever you can do or dream you can, begin it. Boldness has genius, power, and magic in it.

Eventually, an important door opened when she found a way to sell her business and still teach yoga, which is the work she truly loves. Now she can avoid the administrative details and work on her own terms. Before she could do so, she had to let go of the idea that she needed the income from her business to follow her bliss. As we move to listen to the call, to the whispers of our soul, we will, as Thoreau put it, "meet with a success unexpected in common hours."

Consider the following quote:

> The moment one definitely commits oneself, then providence moves too. All sorts of things occur to help one that would never have otherwise occurred. A whole stream of events issues from the decision, raising in one's favor all manner of unforeseen incidents and meetings and material assistance which no one could have dreamed would come [one's] way. Whatever you can do, or dream you can, begin it. Boldness has genius, power and magic in it.
>
> —ASCRIBED TO WOLFGANG GOETHE

Even though in this chapter you will be putting aside your financial data for the moment, know that you are moving forward with a new understanding of your financial picture and your responses to it. With the confidence this understanding gives you, you are now ready to spend some time focusing on your soul's direction.

In the Moment

Life, both the visible and invisible, happens in the moment. Inspiration, grace, God, access to the universal source—all this and more happens right *now*. And we respond with all our history, inclinations, and potential of our being. The beauty of it is that each moment holds infinite possibility. As the poet Emily Dickinson said, "I live in possibility."

The beauty of it is that each moment holds infinite possibility.

A friend once told me that I seemed like Lot's wife: "Rosemary, you are always looking backward." I became indignant and argued with her. But she pointed out how many times I got stuck because I was recounting the past or reliving it. It seemed as though what had happened to me took precedence over what was happening.

Then I began to experiment with the notion of accepting life as my teacher—in each minute of the day, in good ones and rough ones. Each day brought new opportunities to see myself more clearly, to walk intentionally, seeking direction from the moment.

Each morning I began to ask for the grace to live the day consciously with awareness of events and people as a part of a much larger pattern. As I let myself become aware of the enormous power of the present moment, my inner and outer worlds entered a transformative process, and my calling in life became more obvious to me. The clues were all around me, and they began to form a thread that wove its way through my life. Seemingly by happenstance, I learned of the Ministry of Money organization, became a volunteer, and accepted the director's invitation to go to Haiti. When the invitation came, I allowed my intuition to answer for me, instead of listening to all the practical questions and objections in my head. That first trip turned out to be one of the most profound experiences of my life, and a major turning point. Imagine if I hadn't listened! There is a direct link between my finding the Ministry of Money, going to Haiti, and later establishing the independent organization Women's Perspective and directing its current work.

"Doing this work gives validity to my dreams and leads me towards their realization in a practical sense. I have wanted to write children's stories all my life. Now I see a way I can do this."

—A WORKSHOP PARTICIPANT

All these possibilities were contained in the moment I began to live intentionally, cultivating a connection to my soul. This is why I consider my work a divine assignment. My life is energized, encouraged, and uplifted by the extraordinary moments large and small that inevitably arise each day. I encourage you to follow your inner knowing, because I can assure you there is adventure, challenge, satisfaction, and delight in answering your call and fulfilling your potential. Through living your own version of an intentional life, you can:

- Acknowledge who you are.

- Express gratitude for the resources you have.

- Experience your feelings.

- Recognize what you're drawn to.

- Hold the truth of yourself clearly.

- Be aware of what you are currently doing.

- Actively ask for guidance.

- Be fully present to the gifts of the moment.

Discovering Your Call

In the lives of women I have worked with, and in the course of my own life, I have seen amazing transformations happen around the issues of money. Each woman approaches that transformation from a different place. Some are poised to put their money in alignment with their spirit and need only a little "nudge," a little more insight, a new sense of order, to make the connection. Others have more work to do and find that they need more time to understand their finances before they can merge its uses with their spiritual energy.

But over and over, I have seen one consistent pattern: when people allow a dream to come to light, amazing "coincidences" do happen. Perhaps the best way to illustrate this is to tell brief stories of women who changed their lives by heeding a notion, a message, or a messenger.

Accidents Happen

I'll start with my daughter, Sharon Williams. She arrived at her sense of purpose literally by accident. At the end of a cross-country bicycle trip, she was seriously injured in an accident. The trip had been planned during a hiatus from college, at a time when she was looking for a career. She never expected a career to come out of the pain and trauma of a head-and-neck injury.

After she fell over the handlebars and hit her head, she was taken to a hospital. While she was unconscious on the physical plane, she had an inner experience in which she recalls meeting with a group whom she recognized as a spiritual "Board of Advisers." At that moment, she felt she was given a choice to live and she made the commitment to healing.

As Sharon began to recover, she found she was not getting enough pain relief from the usual medical treatments available to her. That's when she went to an excellent chiropractor. Not only did she improve, she found her call: to enter the healing profession as a chiropractor.

As with many choices of the heart, the reality of money, finances, and the demands of the external world entered the picture. Sharon did not have the money to finish college and go on to graduate school to study to be a chiropractor. She knew the issue of financial insecurity all too well. She had seen first her father, then me, lose our "secure" corporate jobs.

But when a chosen path is in alignment with your soul, a way starts to emerge. Sharon found her way through borrowing money for school, finding and buying a small house that was financed with a home equity loan I took out, renting out rooms to pay the loan, and supporting herself with the rental income, while living there herself.

Although she continued to feel the heavy weight of taking on so much debt to complete graduate training, the accident and its aftermath made her more willing to take risks. After her experience in the hospital, she knows firsthand that she is a spiritual being who is here with a purpose: to serve in a healing profession. Her commitment freed her to have the confidence to take on debt and to take steps to pay it back.

Sharon is now a chiropractor with a successful practice She has increasing equity in her own little home. She is now married, expecting her first child, and learning to apply what she has learned to family finances. All the while she is fulfilling her dream, experiencing the honor and privilege of helping people be healthier, in both body and spirit. It is a joy that helps sustain her own family physically and spiritually.

A Story of Faith

I turn now to the story of Anne Hastings. In her own words, Anne has said that she was experiencing a nagging sense that there must be more to life, a longing for more meaning. Rather than disregard that pull, Anne started to think about the Peace Corps and mentioned this to friends. Someone suggested she contact a Haitian priest, Father Joseph Philippe. Father Joseph had a vision of starting a grassroots banking system in Haiti, and he had a dream that he could enlist someone who spoke French, Creole, and English; was a bank president or director; and could volunteer to work for three years in Haiti without pay.

Although Anne could not speak French or Creole, had no banking experience, and needed financial support in order to do a single volunteer year in Haiti, Father Philippe still believed she was the right person. For her part, Anne said, "It just felt right." Funding for her first year came from friends of both Father Philippe and Anne who were intrigued by the idea. She eventually found second-year funding by applying for grants to the San Carlos Foundation in

Berkeley, California, which funds professionals to provide health and educational assistance in third-world countries.

Anne has been in Haiti since 1996. Fonkoze, an alternative bank for Haiti's rural poor, which she helped create, is up and running. And Fondwa, a model rural development community in the mountains of Haiti, is a visible manifestation of her and Father Philippe's intangible dreams.

Among the many surprises along the way for Anne was that, when she entered this path, she did not have a vocabulary of faith. She was not particularly religious and the initial actions that led her to Haiti were not faith-based. She was primarily interested in simplifying her life. Now, after her amazing experiences, she speaks of the strong faith she has gained, learning "to let problematic things go, knowing answers will come."

A Creative Process

My third story is about a woman named Charlotte Lyman Fardelmann. Her life is a beautiful example of how just one person's changed relationship to money can affect many others.

A major financial fact in Charlotte's life was an inheritance that gave her a financial cushion. She felt an overriding discomfort, even guilt, over having more money and resources than the people around her. Where was the justice in that, she wondered?

Charlotte went from feeling isolated from others because she didn't share their money issues, to joining hands with other women who had also inherited money. Together they started the Lyman Fund, which gives small grants to applicants to take the next step on their spiritual journeys.

By having her own fund, Charlotte is not just an observer of the process of change, but a participant in making a difference through the use of money. So far, more than three hundred people have received grants from the Lyman Fund. Each year recipients are invited to a gathering to talk about the changes in their lives since receiving the grants. A community has begun among them, creating more spiritual energy. Her book, *Nudged by the Spirit: Stories of People Responding to the Still, Small Voice of God*, tells the story of the dreams that have come to fruition with the help of seed money.

The catalyst for Charlotte was twofold: the work she did on her money issues and the work she did on her spiritual quest. Through study, workshops, and interaction with others who were focusing on a deeper understanding of money, she overcame her anxiety and transformed her thinking about her inheritance and the power it gave her. And through a prayerful and dedicated study within her faith community of Quakers, she found grounding for her spiritual journey as well as friends who worked with her to create the Lyman Fund. She describes her journey as a five-step creative process. You may find that her steps resonate with yours:

Five-Step Creative Process

1. **Input**: "My childhood discomfort with the wealthy society world."

2. **Gestation**: "Wrestling with the issue of money, learning about people's spiritual journeys, culminating with joining with my two friends to form the Lyman Fund."

3. **Sharing**: "The first seven years of grant giving."

4. **Going Public**: "Celebrating with the grantees as Lyman Fund becomes an incorporated foundation."

5. **Moving On**: "Into the unknown, the beginning of the next cycle in the spiral."

She Wouldn't Take No for an Answer

The woman whose image was put on the Irish five-pound note is Catherine McAuley, the nineteenth-century founder of the Sisters of Mercy, an order of Catholic nuns. She started the order in her forties after she inherited what would be a million dollars today from a childless couple she had befriended. Wanting to use her resources to help the poor of Dublin, she enlisted friends to aid her in bringing food and clothing to people who needed it.

The church authorities at the time told her she couldn't serve the poor because only nuns were allowed to do it. I like to imagine her saying to herself, "Okay, then I'll start an order of nuns. That's how we will get this work of helping the poor accomplished." Catherine's order remains in existence today, continuing the work she started.

There are many things that impress me about this story, including the fact that Catherine McAuley is one of the only women, except for royalty, whose face has ever appeared on a bill. In her case, a life spent integrating financial resources and spiritual values penetrated through to one of the main symbols of the power of money: the actual paper used as currency.

Synergy

The story of Julie Spahr is an example of the kind of synergy that can happen when two women living out their dream come together. Julie had decided to go back to college in midlife to get her degree. She found it such a profound experience that she went on to complete a master's degree program at Temple University. It was an experience that launched a new career for her. Out of her desire to share her enthusiasm for education with other midlife women who dreamed of going back to school for advanced degrees, she included funding for scholarships as a goal for the donor-advised fund she set up through a local community foundation.

Parallel to Julie's story is the story of Elin Danien, a woman who had enrolled as a freshman at the University of Pennsylvania in her midforties. She went on to complete a PhD program and founded a scholarship fund in 1986 named Bread Upon the Waters. This fund grants scholarship money to women over thirty who want to complete an undergraduate degree through part-time study. She personally funded the first scholarship award in 1987. Julie met Elin and heard the inspiring stories of women who had graduated with the help of this program. She became one of their donors. When their purposes came together, these two women were able to create and participate in something larger than either one of them could have done by herself.

What Is Your Work History?

Call grows out of our personal history, the composite of who we are in the world and the experiences we have had. To get a clearer picture, you may find it helpful to take an inventory of your work history, by itemizing all the jobs you have ever had, both paid and unpaid. Here's an example from a workshop participant:

- Household chores
- Pulling weeds
- Cookie maker for Chowder Man
- Baby sitting
- Food server and cashier at Howard Johnson highway rest stop
- Student receptionist at a dorm
- Waitress at a country club
- Office support for director of Women's Studies Department

- Banking: cash management/telephone transfers/filing
- Internship at Arco Chemical Corporate Affairs Department
- Historic house renovation
- Cocktail waitress
- Motel housecleaner (one day)
- Senior Fellow, Dance Department—production of spring dance show
- Management training Meridian Bank
- Office management and accounting for a real estate development company
- Owned and operated a real estate and property management company
- President of Neighborhood Association
- Secretary of Community Historic Preservation Trust
- Committee for University Medical Review Board
- Block captain of Neighborhood Crime Watch Association
- Owned and operated a Laundromat
- Stay-at-home mom (two years)
- Controller at a telecommunications company
- Preschool Sunday School teacher
- Accounting manager for a large mechanical contracting company
- Accounting for husband's distribution business

The point of this exercise is to understand your work history in a new light and to begin to identify your patterns of working. It shows you a lot of things. Do you just take jobs to earn money, are you working to develop a talent, or are you fulfilling a niche? Do you accept a job the way it is, or do you expand it? Do you feel "lucky" in getting jobs, or do you feel it's been a struggle for you to find good work? In essence look for the patterns, feelings, and attitudes expressed in your work history. This should include your significant volunteer work.

My Work History

1. **Now try this exercise for yourself. Make a list of all the jobs—paid or unpaid—that you have done in your life.**

2. **When you finish summarizing your work history, ask yourself the following questions, making notes next to specific jobs, as appropriate.**

   ◆ Was the salary commensurate with the work? Were you overpaid, underpaid, or not paid at all?

   ◆ Did you enjoy the work?

   ◆ What was your motivation for doing the work?

   ◆ Is there a pattern to your work history that stands out for you?

   ◆ Is there any sense of call in this history?

   ◆ Did you make independent decisions based on your own judgment? Or did you pursue a career because you thought you were supposed to?

   ◆ Did you ever create your own job?

   ◆ Have you ever seen a need and designed a way to fill it?

   ◆ Did you start your own business?

What Is Your Spiritual History?

Certainly a key part of who we are is what we believe in, what motivates us on an inner level. Completing the following spiritual history allowed this workshop participant to see the progression and development of her spiritual approach to life.

   ◆ Raised in a strict Catholic household.

   ◆ Attended Catholic school through high school.

   ◆ Lived in a community where everyone was Catholic and church was the center of social life.

- Wanted to be a nun for many years.

- Never met a Jewish person or a Protestant until moving to a suburban community in adolescence.

- Developed many friendships with Jewish girls in middle school.

- Went to a secular college in a large city over the objections of the nuns but with support of family.

- As a freshman in college, went to church and followed Catholic traditions.

- Stopped attending church by the end of my freshman year.

- Learned about Buddhism/Hinduism/Islam in college courses.

- Traveled to countries with other religions.

- Developed an affinity for Eastern traditions.

- Have not returned to Catholicism and did not raise children as Catholics, though still consider myself a member of Catholic tradition.

- Now study metaphysics as a spiritual discipline.

My Spiritual History

Here are some questions to help you take a look at your spiritual history.

1. What does spirituality mean to you?

2. **Do you see yourself as a spiritual person?**

3. **Answer the following questions if you were raised in a spiritual tradition.**

   In what spiritual tradition did your parents train you?

   What are your memories of attending rituals or services as a child?

   Did you get anointed or honored in any celebrations as a child?

   Do you retain your childhood faith today?

Have you changed your belief system?

If so, what motivated the change and when?

Have you adopted new spiritual practices?

If so, what are they?

What are the insights you feel you received from the spiritual beliefs/practices you were raised with?

What issues of life have you explored through a spiritual lens?

4. **Answer the following questions if you were not raised in a spiritual tradition.**

Was spirituality totally absent in your life growing up?

Were you given messages that anything spiritual was unacceptable or even ridiculous?

Do you recall inklings or experiences that gave you a sense of a divine being or a spiritual existence?

At what point did you begin to ask questions about the unseen?

Key Points

Take another moment and summarize for yourself any key points that have emerged as you have reviewed your work/volunteer history and your spiritual history.

Work History

1.

2.

3.

Spiritual History

1.

2.

3.

Being in a Receptive Mode

I consider being in a state of grace as being open to inspiration, intuition, and guidance, and through that openness gaining the ability to transform energy into action. Grace in action manifests as being gracious to myself and to all who are present in my day. I define graciousness as being in a receptive mode. Graciousness isn't a synonym for "nice." Rather it is about being relaxed, an-ticipating good, releasing the need to feel I have to defend myself against the world. When I'm in a gracious mode, my shoulders don't tense, my back doesn't hurt.

Living in a receptive mode means never deeming a time in your life as "outside the plan" or insignificant. It means accepting each stage of growth as important and all events as valuable. It means being open to hearing the call. Again, it is living in the now.

Graciousness means holding your hand open rather than walking around with a clenched fist. It means answering the doorbell with a receptivity to whomever might be calling instead of arriving at the door irritated at being bothered.

Living in a receptive mode means never deeming a time in your life as "outside the plan" or insignificant. It means accepting each stage of growth as important and all events as valuable. It means being open to hearing the call. Again, it is living in the now.

There is so much "noise" in the lives of people in industrialized countries: commitments, work, family, television, computers, radios, advertisements, reading material, telephones, cell phones, pagers, vacations. How can we possibly hear a spiritual call in the midst of all this?

To hear your call over the din of daily demands, you need to allow yourself to be in a listening posture, in a receptive mode. Many women I know have built silence into their routines a few mornings a week or part of one day each month. One thing I do know: To bring silence into your life, you need to put it on your calendar. Silence doesn't usually happen by accident.

When you are silent, ask yourself: what am I hearing today? Be open. Let the answers come, now or later. You don't need to force them; they have their own energy. As women, we seem to be always trying to do so much. Don't *do* . . . *be*. And you will begin to feel the motion of direction.

Paying Attention

Although some people may describe their "call" as coming in a lightning bolt or as a stunning revelation, for most of us, call comes one step at a time, bit by bit. We have a sense, we pursue an interest, we follow an inner knowing and in due time, our call begins to take shape.

I think of Beth Eliason, a woman whom I met by chance at a conference—even though a mutual friend had been trying to get us together for months. Beth had always felt a strong pull to the culture and language of China. Her attraction persisted through marriage, being a mother, doing community service, and going back to college. In the course of her explorations, she saw a video about a convent in China. When she later took a trip to China with the Waterbury Chorale of Waterbury, Connecticut, it happened that one of the tour guides was a student of the superior of the order of Buddhist nuns she had seen on the video. That guide helped set Beth's dream in motion, and she is now going to teach English as a second language to the very same convent of Buddhist nuns she had seen in the video. Exceeding even her wildest expectations, she has been asked by the superior of the convent to serve the nuns as a bridge between Buddhism and Christianity. By paying attention to her interest, by allowing herself to follow the thread that emerged, Beth is living out her dream.

What Calls to You?

A call can come through a talent, a strong desire, an urge, or a notion. We often see a call in motion in a singer, dancer, ball player, swimmer, or an artist. We most often notice call in others when they forsake the usual path and embark on a new, riskier path, or pursue an idea that goes counter to prevailing attitudes. As the boomer generation ages, I am reading articles that say many in this age group are leaving highly paid jobs to become spiritual leaders—ministers, rabbis, or Buddhist teachers.

However, a call can also be seen in the motion of daily living: the desire to stay home to raise children rather than leave the home to work . . . the interest in making a healthy meal several nights a week rather than eating out of a box . . . the quiet resolve to scour the shelves of the local library to find pleasing or inspiring books . . . the goal to live a life of harmony just where you are, surrounded and supported by small signs of peace—a lighted candle, a warm soup, a hearty laugh. Or it can mean changing everything, starting over.

A call can be an embracing of what is truly available rather than a quest for what's more and different.

In talking with people about the search for their call, I recommend thinking "simple." Sometimes in the quest for more money to buy things, we reject the beauty of the rhythm of life as it can be lived even in the twenty-first century. A call can be an embracing of what is available rather than a quest for what's more and different.

Take some time now to write down what you are sensing for yourself as you focus on this idea of call. You may have just a fragment or small bit of an idea. You may simply be aware of an image or feeling. As you write, let yourself be receptive to whatever comes to you without judgment or qualifiers, without weighing the pros and cons, without discriminating between reality and possibility.

I have been directing you to write many of your responses to the questions posed. This time, try something else and draw your response. Find some markers or crayons and draw any lines, symbols, or shapes that seem to present themselves. In a recent workshop with an artist friend, Janet Slom of Westport, Connecticut, I found that drawing of an impression or a thought was a significant move to understanding a notion just below the surface of consciousness. Explore your responses through color.

Recap

In this chapter you have opened yourself up to some dreams and possibilities. There is one more thing I am going to ask of you—to do nothing. Yes ... you read this correctly. Do nothing. Just sit and let your thoughts come to you.

> In the sweet territory of silence
> we touch the mystery,
> where we can connect with deep knowing.
> —ANGELES ARRIEN

Women are familiar with slow growth. Let this be a time of gestation. This is not the time to hurry yourself or demand a plan. This is the time to hold your thoughts quietly until a clearer vision forms, to nurture your new thoughts. Hold them in a sacred space until they begin to grow and change. Allow them to unfold in their own time.

Observe your curiosity and notice what takes shape. Create the space to let new ideas enter, take hold, and grow. Let your imagination be active. Daydream. As a child, I was told not to daydream, as though it were a bad thing. Now I know that daydreaming is an active ingredient of hearing inner direction.

Pay attention to your nighttime dreams, too. You might want to record them in your journal. When you reread them, it may be easier to hear the messages encoded in your images. If you do begin drawing some of your responses to your life you may find your dreams relate to some of the symbols you draw. The psychotherapist Carl Jung drew mandalas daily for a time and these drawings served as a journal of his life. An artist friend, Clara Wainwright of Boston, Massachusetts, asks her students to draw a self-portrait every day. These are all ways to identify your true self and your life's call.

Let your answers to the questions asked of you in this book flow through the silence into your soul's time and space. Just pay attention!

Chapter Six

Your Action Plan

The Eighth Day of Creation

I believe we are living in the "eighth day of creation." This is a concept used by Elizabeth O'Connor in her book *Cry Pain, Cry Hope* to express the fact that creation continues, and that we are co-creators of ourselves and the future world. We have the responsibility not just to enjoy creation, but to encourage its continual unfolding.

As O'Connor has written, "If we are to make ultimate sense of our lives, all the disparate elements in us have to be integrated around call." The element of money is no exception. I believe that money is a gift, along with the many other resources given in different form and measure to each of us.

And I believe that the money you need to pursue your own path, to achieve your deepest desires, to work for the good of others, is available and can be accessed, albeit in unusual or unexpected ways.

You have begun a money journey that will keep evolving over time. You started with your financial history: your *Money Messages* and your *Money Autobiography*. You moved to recognizing your *Money Facts and Feelings* and creating *Alignment*. And you have considered some of your *Dreams*. You are now ready to move to the sixth stage of The Money Journey Circle: taking *Action*. This is the time to walk into your future by taking intentional steps.

the money journey circle

"True wisdom comes from understanding that the universe is balanced on our actions, each and every one of us. Our understanding of the significance of this mystical fact leads us to an awesome conclusion: Each one of us is responsible for how the universe will unfold."
—David A. Cooper,
God Is a Verb

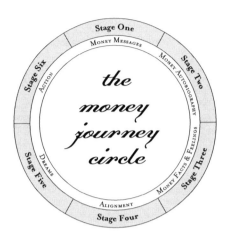

Using Money Consciously

Taking action grows out of knowing what is important to you and deciding how you will use your means toward the ends you truly desire. The actions you decide to take may not be big ones. You may decide to change just small things at first. For example, you might skip buying lattes for an entire month, a choice that will put an additional $90 ($3 x thirty days) into your pocket. You recognize that this choice is not really a sacrifice, because home-brewed coffee tastes just as good to you! What will you do with that newfound $90? That's where alignment comes in. Perhaps you've recognized that it is most important to you to reduce your credit card debt and you apply the $90 to your payment each month. Or perhaps you want to do something concrete for others and you find an organization that can use your $90 to fund a year's schooling for a child in a developing country.

"You are here to enable the divine purpose of the universe to unfold. That is how important you are!"

—ECKHART TOLLE,
The Power of Now

This is the beginning of becoming more conscious and intentional about how you use your resources. For example, I don't think I need another sheet or towel in my life. But each time I see those "white sales" advertised, I want to run out and buy more. Why? I can't resist the idea of getting fresh linens at half price! It's a habit, but I don't need any more linens. Instead of automatically responding out of habit, I can choose to stop and think through whether that $50, $75, $100, $500 or more could be used with far more satisfaction in a different way. What if I were to give it as a gift to someone who needs it? Or contribute it to a community activity? Or invest it in another share of stock? Or buy a theater ticket to a play I wanted to see but felt was too much of an indulgence?

Ask yourself whether you feel deprived of what you desire. Does this sense of deprivation relate to having many things you really don't desire or need? Do you acquire things driven by impulse because you live in a society defined by consumer goods?

As we expand the discussion on helping others in the world, you may be wondering, "Do I have to put my own economic needs aside for the sake of compassion for others?" If that thought makes you uncomfortable, phrase the question another way: "What can I do to support myself without ignoring the needs of others who have less or need help?" My answer is to use your money consciously. By making intentional choices, I believe you can nourish both yourself and others. You can resolve the conflicts in your heart and your pocketbook over how to be a caretaker of your own needs and a good citizen of the world. In effect, I think you have to take care of yourself in order to take care of others. And I believe you can do both, even with limited resources. What prevents you from achieving this wholeness is the fragmentation that comes from a consumer mindset of "buy, buy, buy for me, me me." Resist impulses and habitual actions. Open yourself to connecting to your core. Welcome the experience of listening to your intuition. I think you will find the universe responds by opening ways for you to do so. You will be able to develop the habit of intuitive action, rather than impulse buying!

Let me give you an example from my own life. One of my joys is to send greeting cards. I often used to come home with $20 or $30 worth of greeting cards. Now, I buy cards that support a cause or that are handmade by a women's cooperative in a developing country. I can still send a message of love, sympathy, or congratulations

> *"What is now becoming very important to me is to actively to take part in shaping this world as a woman, to know the power of myself and my resources, and to act to improve my life and to reach out to other women."*
>
> —A WORKSHOP PARTICIPANT

149

—but now it has added meaning. Because I enjoy the luxury of sending a lovely note, an organization that helps the world benefits!

This kind of shift has happened over and over in my life, thanks to my growing awareness and commitment to enact my values. I now use the library more rather than buying expensive books. I often use the cash I save to buy books for people who have no other resources to get them. I love to be with friends, and now instead of preparing time-consuming elegant dinners myself, I invite groups of friends to potluck suppers at my home. Inevitably these turn into happy events with people sharing their own lovingly prepared favorite dishes!

I offer these simple examples to you because I want to illustrate in a very concrete, basic way how changing your patterns and your focus around money will not deprive you. It will enhance you!

I think satisfaction eludes us when we act out of misalignment. We're left with a feeling that there is never enough money. Satisfaction comes from tapping into our core—spirit, soul, psyche, heart—and from acknowledging our material resources and using them wisely and intentionally. Acting out of financial and spiritual alignment is a liberating experience, one that asks you to reach for or create what you want by using what you have.

In my work with women I have noticed a curious disabling effect when women feel they need permission to do something for themselves or give away money to what they believe in. This happens especially when women consider making larger donations than usual or making a significant step on their own behalf, like recognizing they need to go back to graduate school to fulfill a career dream. The impact of the decision and the amount of money seems to paralyze some women, even when they know they can afford it! It is important to acknowledge this need for permission, as well as to uncover its source. This need can inhibit true alignment until it is recognized and acknowledged.

Vision

I believe that the way we spend money does make a difference. In the very act of using money we are casting a vote, and our voice creates a powerful vibration in our own lives and beyond. It reaches the political arena; the manufacturing and service sectors; our spiritual centers, schools, and universities; and our families and communities. It is a blessing that brings creative energy into a new place.

By adding our vision as women, we are complementing what has been until now a predominantly male-oriented vision in most societies. Our voices, our choices, our actions, and yes, our money, is needed for the fullness of the world. How much we as women can contribute!

> *"Woman ... daring to think and move and speak—to undertake to help shape, mold and direct the thought of her age, is merely completing the circle of the world's vision."*
> —ANNA JULIA COOPER,
> *A Voice from the South*

Words Are Action

Talking about money is one of the hardest "actions" that women have to take. I believe this goes back to our cultural messages and histories. Is money talk unladylike, uncomfortable, unnatural, unimportant, unnecessary, or just impossible?

My answer is no! Money talk is as much a subject for women as how to raise a child, roast a chicken, or choose an outfit. It's just that we've been prevented from making it as natural and comfortable as any one of those typical "female" subjects. It is time to change that attitude because talking about money is vitally important and necessary—and entirely possible. The process can be eye-opening, and the result? Enriching!

I will give you a recent example. Several months ago I gave a workshop at a religious institution for which I was to be paid a certain fee. As always with my work, I did a lot of preparation, traveled to the event, and put all my energy into being totally present and engaged at the time of the conference.

There was some confusion over whether my fee was to be paid out of the budget of the department that had invited me or the institution's central budget. I made several calls back and forth. And waited.

Months later, I still had not received my fee. Now, have you ever had a plumber leave your house without a check? Or have you ever gone into a store, picked out an item, and walked out the door, saying "I'll pay later?" Yet, we accept delays in payments for our services, or fees that don't adequately compensate for our time and efforts—often silently.

Finally, the department acknowledged its responsibility and said it would send the fee at the end of the current month—now several months past the time I had performed the work. I could have remained silent or replied with a simple "thank you" as I fumed over the unfairness of the situation. But I've worked enough on my money journey that I came right back with, "No, I want the money sent to me now."

The response? It was not horror, anger, disapproval, insult—whatever criticisms we fear we will get (and maybe feel we deserve) when we speak up. The answer was, okay, we will send it this week. End of story.

What does this have to do with spirituality? Everything. Spirituality is about manifesting our values and our core beliefs in the world. One of our deepest values is our own self-worth. If we don't value ourselves, how can we truly value each other? After all, we are all one. Speaking up about money—the tangible acknowledgement of value—emboldens us to speak up about our other core issues. For example, if we see an injustice in our community, we need to be clear that it is our right to speak out and that it is natural to do so. Silencing ourselves about money can repress our instincts about value, justice, and equity.

Express Yourself about Money

What is one difficult area for you in talking about money?
(For example, asking for a raise; talking to your partner or
spouse about spending; setting a price for your work with a
client; telling your children there isn't money to pay for something they want.)

**What do you think would happen if you raised the subject with
directness? List three dire consequences you can imagine:**

Now list three positive outcomes you can imagine:

Create a dialogue that has a positive outcome. What would you say? What would the other person say? Go back and forth until you've explored all the issues, the anger, the discomfort. Use your imagination. End on a "winning" note.

Now use the dialogue you've created and go out and have the actual conversation! In fact, practice by talking about money in lots of ways and circumstances. Bring the topic up with your bank (how about reducing those fees?), with your family, in conversation with friends. Make money talk natural in your life.

Granted, money has its own language (jargon) and most of us don't have time anymore to learn a new language. Why? Because we're too busy earning money and then spending it on all the consumer items we think we need today! What's missing is direct conversation about the various money issues that affect our lives. Go into these conversations knowing what you want to say and then say it without emotional overtones. If necessary, write down what you want to say ahead of time, or rehearse with a friend. A good conversation about money can indeed feed your soul.

Salespeople, advertisers, product designers, and market researchers all know about the power of women as consumers, and they are hard at work redirecting our money to their ends. I do not hold any hostility toward these companies and their employees. They are businesses after all and they hold up the economy. Salespeople and market researchers work hard and have families to support. Our challenge is not to stop functioning in a consumerist, capitalist society that competes at every moment for our money. Our challenge is to live in this world without getting sucked in to its excesses, to maintain own integrity in the face of multiple demands for our dollar.

The materialistic focus of our society simply makes it that much harder to make choices that are in line with who we really are and what we want to create. With all the noise of the external communicators, it can be almost impossible at times to hear the still, small voice of our inner messenger.

Bringing our financial values and our spiritual vision together means understanding our resources and being intentional about our choices. It allows us to operate from a place of fulfillment, so we have the energy not just to make our own lives hum, but also to contribute to the possibilities of others. It aligns us with the energy of synchronicity.

One example of this kind of synchronicity is the Holly Wheeler Fund. You've never heard of that fund? I'm not surprised. It was started by a friend of mine for herself. Holly and I were sitting on the beach one day as she talked about wanting to go back to school to receive training as a psychotherapist. But—and this may sound very familiar—she didn't have the money.

I replied, "Why don't you ask friends and family to help you?"

Her immediate response was, "Oh, I can't do that."

And I said, "Of course you can." And I gave her a check for ten dollars to begin the Holly Fund.

Now that contribution was only meant as a symbol, and certainly it would not help much, but it did serve to jump-start her ability to get to school. I was so inspired by her enthusiasm to begin a new career that I made a gesture. And in that gesture, she saw the possibility that somehow, from somewhere, the money would come if she followed her dream.

I recently got a letter from Holly in which she said, "I would never have taken the plunge without your 'of course you can do this' encouragement." She applied to the institute that she was interested in attending and pursued the Holly Fund as a creative way to generate the money she needed. By the way, five years later, Holly is now a therapist following her chosen path.

I think we all have the ability to listen, to take a step, and to empower people. It doesn't take much. Even ten dollars will do. One woman, working with others and using the money available to her, can create far-reaching opportunities. Who knows what can spring from such efforts, and when?

Gaining Clarity

Have you ever written a "mission statement" for yourself? Before you let those words intimidate you, think of it this way: "If I could transform just one small bit of my current reality—or the whole thing—what might I be ready to do? Or what might I be ready to begin to think about doing?"

The core of your mission is what is important to you. It might be to start a business or to go back to school. Or to make room in your schedule to bring comfort to an elderly relative on a weekly basis. Or to step out into a more activist role and join forces with an organization that tries to address the problems of the homeless in your city. Maybe you want to create a shift in attitude and tempo, to create more peace and stability in your own home. Don't let your mission be determined by what other people expect of you, or what you might have expected from yourself in the past. This is a whole new era in your life. Give yourself some time to consider these next two questions:

What are some specific things that are important to you at this time in your life?

What actions could you take to make these things begin to happen? (Schedule a visit to a nursing home? Check out public transportation to learn the bus route to get there? Petition your city representative to pass a bill to construct a homeless shelter? Contribute to a food bank? Introduce one "quiet night" each week? Establish a family night for playing board games?) What you do can be as small as taking a single step, or as large as creating a whole new organization. For example, after participating in a workshop, one woman realized she wanted to teach her daughter about philanthropy and to make her city a better place to live. She created a family foundation with the goal of developing some inner-city projects that would involve her daughter.

Possibilities

Any action plan ultimately needs some specifics, some clear intention to carry it out. But you do not need elaborate plans. Consider specific small changes you might make to get clearer about your call. Here are some decisions other women have told me they have made to get clarity. This is how they expressed their commitments:

- ◆ I will carry a small memo pad with me and make notes in it about my daily financial activities: spending, financial decisions, and feelings.

- ◆ I will meditate for five or ten minutes, starting at 7 a.m., every day for one week. I will follow my meditation with five minutes of journaling about what is next for me on my money journey. Each Sunday morning I will spend fifteen minutes reviewing my journal.

- ◆ I will check out a "debtors anonymous" meeting because I see a problem with debt in my financial picture.

- ◆ I will designate the next four Wednesday nights as "Quiet Nights." There will be no TV or music or computers turned on. I will read or write about my financial concerns and interests.

- ◆ I will start a money and spirituality group, or a book group using this book. I will lead the group.

- ◆ I will give $50, $500, $5,000 to something I find I have passion about. I will do more than write a check; I will tune deeply in to my feelings and make notes in my journal about my feelings at the moment of giving and for as long as the experience of giving resonates with my soul.

- ◆ I will join an investment club.

- ◆ I will create a giving circle.

- ◆ I will interview a financial planner to help me find the resources to take the actions I would like to take.

- ◆ I will take a continuing education course in finances at the local college.

- ◆ I will learn a computer software program that will help me keep track of bills and checks.

- ◆ I will change one financial behavior: For the next month, I will bring a bag lunch and take a walk instead of buying lunch. I will enjoy using the money I save to buy some thing special for myself or someone else.

- ◆ I will check out the business and finance shelves at a bookstore and look for publications that are in tune with my needs and interests.

- ◆ I will go to the library for the next two Thursday evenings from 6 to 7:30 p.m. to do financial research or gather information about my deep interest. I will record what I read and journal about my feelings. I will make this commitment in my calendar and let nothing interfere.

- ◆ I will learn about socially responsible investments.

- ◆ I will continue to seek guidance and inspiration in my financial life.

What will your next steps be? Make some promises to yourself about what you will do to move forward on your money journey and note them here.

Write down the name of one person whom you will share these plans with—someone to whom you can be accountable for carrying them out.

"Bag Lady"

Just the words "bag lady" can inspire fear. I have seen over and over again that, at this stage of "getting real" about possible choices and changes, money fears seem to rise again to the top of many women's list: How much it will cost? Can I earn enough if I do that? Will I have enough money if I make that choice? Will I end up a "bag lady"? When will I run out of money?

These types of "bag lady" fears influence many women: the idea that somehow, if we take charge of our money, if we make choices that follow our heart, we will lose everything and end up on the street in rags, pushing a shopping cart filled with our only belongings. Homelessness is surely an extreme and very sad part of our society, but it is not a likely result for anyone who is seriously coming to grips with finances. Trust me. It's not going to happen. You are going to move slowly. You are going to take things one step at a time.

I do know this: "Bag lady" fears surface most often when money—or the lack of it—is the top priority. And as long as you put money concerns at the head of your list, you will block your path. Your fears will get in the way of the possibilities available to you. It is important to come to grips with your fears about money in order to hear your call clearly.

Consider what you are afraid of: Success? Failure? Being alone? Losing a job? Losing money? Losing the love of a family member? Losing someone's respect? Being sick? War? Fire? Economic downturn? Dying? Someone else dying? Being criticized?

Write down any money fears that come to mind. Don't hold back on naming just what might be keeping you from moving forward.

I am afraid of . . .

Now write down your money fears again, uncensored. Yes, you just did that, but I want you to try again. The first time around you may have filtered out some fears. Remember, fears limit you. Naming your fears may well unlock paralysis in some areas of your life.

I am afraid of . . .

Keep on Keeping On

Sue Roselle did not become penniless when she gave up her high-powered job and returned to Pittsburgh. She found work and a lifestyle in a community that resonated with her spirit.

"Any good that I may do, let me do it now, as I may not pass this way again."

—AN OLD SAYING MY MOTHER

USED TO TELL ME

Anne Hastings did not let the external obstacles of Father Philippe's lack of funds stop her from moving to Haiti, helping start a bank, and finding a deeper meaning for her life.

To fulfill her dream of becoming a chiropractor, Sharon Williams did not give up when there was no apparent money to fund her education. She used borrowed money to achieve her goal of helping people heal, and her success is allowing her to pay back her debt.

Charlotte Fardelmann did not dispose of all her inherited wealth. She took a portion of it and put it together with the contributions of others to provide seed money to fund the dreams of others.

What is the message here? Don't let your fears block your possibilities.

We don't discuss our feelings about money because they make us uncomfortable. These untouched fears can be like unexploded land mines. They have the potential to do you harm if you don't dig them out and release them. *Clearing up a minefield can turn it into a field of possibilities.*

One way to move beyond your fears is to talk about them with people you trust and who are striving for consciousness in their own lives. Talking in a safe place allows your fears to be more vocal and visible. Above all, be patient with yourself. Be kind to yourself. Compliment yourself. You are doing a good job. Keep it up. Made a mistake? Do it over or forget it and just move on. Mistakes are part of the pattern of our lives. Let go of remorse and guilt. Acknowledge how you feel and go on. That is the important part: Keep on keeping on.

Moving Forward

As I revise this book, I think of all the women I have met since writing the first edition, women in Haiti, Guatemala, Mexico, Kenya, and in the halls and meeting rooms of the United Nations. The faces of these women keep showing up on the inner screen of my mind. I know they want the same things for themselves and their children that I do.

I am unsettled by the juxtaposition of their poverty with the prosperity enjoyed by many people around the world. Why is there such inequity? And what can I do about it? After my travels to foreign countries, I cannot simply re-enter my life in the United States without thinking about the marginalized women of the world who have no welfare, public health, or education systems. No cushion of safety exists to provide even the most basic necessities of food and medicine to those who need them so much.

I have watched people try to survive as best they can despite the most difficult conditions. The women band together to help each other, sharing their small measure of food or pooling their little bit of money to buy medicine for one of their children who is sick. They often sing or tell each other stories as they gather. I sense the energy of comradeship even in the middle of the greatest hardships.

As I listen to the questions from women in the United States about what can they do with their lives and their resources, I feel a renewal of my inspiration and my commitment to answer my call: to make a bridge between women here and women in developing countries. I imagine the possibilities of creating new programs.

In my dreams, I see an "Adopt a Mother" program as a way for women to reach out to other women, one-on-one. How little money it would take to make a big difference in another woman's life! A small financial contribution could be a large spiritual contribution for affluent women to make. No big organizations or administrative costs … just one woman "adopting" another, sharing resources and love.

Women's Perspective and its colleagues have begun such a program in a small village in Kenya, on the shores of Lake Victoria. Like many villages in Kenya and throughout Africa, this village has been hard hit by the HIV/AIDS pandemic. When I was there two years ago I met a woman who had organized the HIV/AIDS widows and created small businesses with them. I looked for her again this year and found she had started a new community home-based orphan-care project. I met with her and some of the women who had agreed to care for orphans in addition to caring for their own children. I was so moved by their stories, their determination, and their courage, I offered to find them partners in the United States and to partner with them myself. There is a family in Westport, Connecticut, that heard the story and opened their hearts to help. Currently, we are sending money for school fees, buying a cow, and funding the irrigation of a few fields. Will there be others who join in this effort to help? I hope so.

"We are not called to save the whole world, but we are called to love and care for those put before us be they neighbors far or near."
—CARY SCOTT, A COMPANION ON A TRIP TO HAITI

The experience of call is not a one-time event, like one-stop shopping. It evolves and grows. It is a life-engaging process with its own momentum. It does not exclude the other pleasures and activities of life, but it does have a core place in your life's purpose.

If you worry about money, about how things will work out in your life, you are just being human. But in doing the work of this book, I hope you have experienced another reality too: You don't need to let those worries rule your life. You can work with your history, your current facts, and your deepest soul motivations to mold your life in a different way. And when you have those moments of doubt about the hard facts of reality versus the soft murmuring of the soul, recall these brief words of Ada Maria Isasi-Diaz, a Latina theologian, author, and teacher: "The only way we can move forward is to live the reality we envision."

You Are Your Own Best Resource

One of the most valuable resources you have is ... *you*. Give honor to your process by taking the time to write a summary of your learning and your commitment. As you move on, you can refer to this summary, revise it, use it for meditation, and develop it as a basis for further action.

Important money messages I have identified that have influenced my thinking and behavior:

Important facts from my money autobiography that have influenced my decisions:

My current financial facts are:
  Assets _____
  Liabilities _____
  Net Worth _____

My most recent cash flow reflects:

Income _____

Expenditures _____

Net Cash Flow _____

At the moment, my life work is focused on:

I express my current spiritual life as follows:

The things that feed my soul are:

I am passionate about:

Organizations or projects I would like to support include:

My plans:

Direction(s) I want to keep:

Things I want to change:

Questions or topics I would like to revisit periodically:

Recap

Your personal summary of your *Money Messages*, your *Money Autobiography*, your *Money Facts and Feelings*, *Alignment* with your spiritual vision, your *Dreams*, and your *Actions* can be a valuable tool. Make plans to review it on a periodic basis.

One system that works for some people is to do so on their birthday, anniversary, or other important personal date. Along with the usual rituals of those days, you might want to create a ritual of looking at this summary and updating it, taking into account who you are at that moment in time.

If you have been working with this book in a group, consider scheduling periodic meetings where you can share your updates with the other members. You might also want to consider a project that you could do together. By now, you have shared your fears and dreams in a way that few others have. Use that energy to create something new.

You might also want to take the work that you have done in this book into the world by creating a Money Journey Circle for other women. Circles have always been very important among women throughout the world. If you want to start such a circle, I suggest you refer to Jean Shinoda Bolen's book *The Millionth Circle*.

Clearly your money journey does not end when you put down this book. Here are some ideas about ways to continue your journey:

- Experiment shifting direction by spending your money in a different way, gradually.

- Use some of the thoughts you have written as a source for personal meditation.

- Become more informed about philanthropy. An excellent resource is Tracy Gary's book, *Inspired Philanthropy*.

- Ask yourself some open-ended questions. For example, "What do I need to do about my financial life?"

One of the requests I have heard most often from women as I traveled the country with my book in hand has been, "Tell me more about investing wisely so I can use my money to support positive businesses and organizations. Tell me more about philanthropy so I can learn how to give in ways that go beyond the limitations of simply writing a check." While this subject is far too vast for me to fully address in this book, those requests speak to the natural next step after you've completed this first phase in your journey. Once you have learned to link your spiritual and monetary values, you will want to take your newfound money wisdom out into the wider world though conscious investing and creative philanthropic action.

Even if you are not yet ready to consider yourself a philanthropist or to become an engaged socially responsible investor, I encourage you to explore the options open to you. For example, you can consider the following:

- ◆ Create or join a giving circle or a discussion group on investing.

- ◆ Research companies before you invest so you choose ones that are compatible with your values.

- ◆ Visit your nearest community foundation or women's fund office to learn about their activities and to see if you want to participate.

- ◆ Become more informed about philanthropy.

- ◆ Consider joining a social activist group that stands for a cause you believe in.

- ◆ Take some small step to solidify your resolve; for instance, read a book on the following resource list. Just get going on your new path.

You might be far more ready than you think. No matter where you are now in your journey, open the door to possibility so that whenever you are ready, the pathway will already be illuminated for you.

A Psalm for Midwives

This last section of the book has focused on the wide variety of ways in which women have identified their dreams, heard a call, and taken action to begin a new life's work. You have been asked to become aware of the presence of dreams in your life, and you are being challenged to take the next step.

The *Action* stage of your money journey is a stage of vulnerability. As you explore new ideas and experiment with new actions, you will be taking risks. You may face new challenges, you may get discouraged, you may experience times of excitement. As you move forward on your journey, hold this thought in your mind: As I birth my dreams into actions, I am midwifing my future. *Be open to the power of creation in the next step, the frightening, seemingly impossible, experience of birthing.*

The metaphor of midwife has always had special resonance for women and is beautifully expressed in the following psalm by Miriam Therese Winter, a member of the Medical Mission Sisters in Hartford, Connecticut, who is well-known as a song writer, author, and leader in feminist spirituality. Read it slowly and take it to heart for your journey.

"A Psalm for Midwives"
by Miriam Therese Winter

Choir 1
You will know
when it is time
to bring to birth
the new creation.

Choir 2
The signs
will be all around you,
urging, insisting:
now is the time.

Choir 1
You have to know
just when to bear down
and concentrate
on one thing only.

Choir 2
It takes labor,
hard, hard labor
to bring forth something new.

All
Be Midwife to our dreams, Shaddai.
Make midwives of us all.

Choir 1
You have to know
just when to push
for something that is
worth fighting for.

Choir 2
If you push too soon,
the dream,
so close to fulfillment,
may be stillborn.

Choir 1
You have to know
how hard to push
when something new
is about to happen.

Choir 2
If you push too hard,

you may be too exhausted
or too discouraged
to continue on,
or someone may step in
to stop you,
causing you to abort.

All
Be Midwife to our hopes, Shaddai.
Make midwives of us all.

Choir 1
You have to know
how to cut the cord
and how to let go
of what has been;

Choir 2
for what will be
will be different
and it will take some time
to adjust.

Choir 1
You have to know
how to wait
for things to settle
after the dream is born,

Choir 2
and how to handle
the consequences—
clean up the mess
and then move on.

All
Be Midwife to our freedom, Shaddai.
Make midwives of us all.

Choir 1
How good it is
to bring to birth.

Choir 2
or to help another
bring to birth.

Choir 1
How good it is
to deliver the dream.

Choir 2
Let us nurture it
to fulfillment.

All
Be Midwife to the future, Shaddai.
Make midwives of us all.

(Note: In this song, the word "Shaddai" comes from the Hebrew and is considered a name for the female aspect of God, sometimes translated as "the breasted one.")

A Parting Gift

Regardless of where your dreams take you, I hope you have completed this book with a new and deep appreciation for your history, your resources, your power, and your spiritual life. In closing, I want to offer you the following Tenets of a Spiritual Money Journey. You might want to post these in a place where you can refer to them often as you continue your money journey. They can serve as a source of encouragement, reminding you of your goals, and keeping you in touch with the reasons why you embarked on this money journey in the first place.

Remember: Every possibility is open to you.

Tenets of a Spiritual Money Journey

- To see money as one of the gifts in your life.

- To recognize the difference between your needs and your wants.

- To stay clear about your "response-ability" in relation to the money you have earned, inherited, or been given.

- To pray and reflect on what you truly want to do with that money.

- To clarify how you will share, use, save, invest, or spend that money wisely.

- To base your financial decisions on your inner voice, rather than a message from the past.

- To be aware of whose agenda you're following: your ego's, someone else's, or the agenda of a higher purpose.

- To view your use of money in the context of your whole life, keeping your financial transactions in alignment with your spiritual values.

Many book groups use this book as the basis for working together on their own money journey process. We have developed a Leadership Guide that gives step-by-step directions on starting and leading a book group. We have also created additional exercises to offer in the group as you proceed through the chapters in the book. These new exercises amplify and enhance the process.

If you would like this material, which is available for a small fee, please contact:

E-mail: info@womensperspective.org

Mail: Women's Perspective
421 Meadow Street
Fairfield, CT 06824

Phone: 203-336-2238

Fax: 203-336-2240

Resources

Chapters One and Two

Benson, Herbert, MD, and Miriam Z. Klipper. *The Relaxation Response.* New York: William Morrow, 1975, revised Harper Torch, 2000. Reference for treating the harmful effects of stress.

Bolen, Jean Shinoda, MD. *Goddesses in Everywoman.* New York: HarperCollins, 1984. A new psychology of women.

Myss, Carolyn. *Anatomy of the Spirit: The Seven Stages of Power and Healing.* New York: Crown Publishing, 1996. A description of the relationship between the physical, energetic, and spiritual systems of a human being.

O'Connor, Elizabeth. *Cry Pain, Cry Hope: Thresholds to Purpose.* Waco, TX: Word Books, 1987. A guide to the dimensions of call.

O'Connor, Elizabeth. *Our Many Selves.* New York: HarperCollins, 1971. (This book is out-of-print but worth it if you can find it.) A handbook to self-discovery.

Pert, Candace B., PhD. *Molecules of Emotion: Why You Feel the Way You Feel.* New York: Scribner, 1997. Information on cellular memory.

Teilhard de Chardin, Pierre. *The Divine Milieu.* New York: HarperCollins, 1960. Explains how we can enter into cooperative activity with God, making our spiritual life part of the continuing evolution of the universe.

Tolle, Eckhart. *The Power of Now.* Novato, CA: New World Library, 1999. Guide to spiritual enlightenment.

Wheatley, Margaret J. *Leadership and the New Science: Discovering Order in a Chaotic World*. San Francisco: Berrett-Koehler, 1999. An understanding of chaos as a necessary part of organization and growth.

Wheatley, Margaret J. *Turning to One Another*. San Francisco: Berrett-Koehler, 2002. Conversations to restore hope to the future.

Chapters Three and Four

Books

Gardner, David, and Tom Gardner. *The Motley Fool Investment Guide: How the Fools Beat Wall Street's Wise Men and How You Can Too*. New York: Fireside, 1996, 2001. A guide to investing based on the theories of the Gardner brothers, authors who use the "Motley Fool" image—a court jester who is the only individual in the royal court who can get away with telling the king the truth—as a symbol of their humorous straight talk about money.

Gardner, David, and Tom Gardner. *The Motley Fool Investment Workbook*. New York: Fireside, 1998, 2001. Charts, graphs, questionnaires, and quizzes to help investors identify resources and develop investment strategies. (Motley Fool materials are also available on tape.)

Korten, David C. *When Corporations Rule the World*. Bloomfield, CT: Kumarian Press, and San Francisco: Berrett-Koehler, 1995, 2001. This book explores the emerging global system of business as a threat to human beings.

Meeker-Lowery, Susan. *Invested in the Common Good*. Philadelphia, PA, and Gabriola Island, British Columbia: New Society

Publishers, 1995. An excellent introduction to socially conscious investing.

Nemeth, Maria, PhD. *The Energy of Money*. New York: Ballantine, 1997. A good resource book for those who want to explore personal motivations regarding money management.

Needleman, Jacob. *Money and the Meaning of Life*. New York: Currency Doubleday, 1991, 1994. A philosopher offers interesting thoughts on the philosophy underlying the use of money.

Nouwen, Henri J. M. *Life of the Beloved: Spiritual Living in a Secular World*. New York: Crossroad, 1992. A remarkable aspect of this book is that while Nouwen is writing to a personal friend, he uses a language that speaks clearly and convincingly to all who search for the spirit of God in the world.

Orman, Suze. *The 9 Steps to Financial Freedom*. New York: Crown Publishers, 1997, 2000. This book provides good basic financial-planning information.

Financial Newsletters

Green Money Journal
PO Box 67
Santa Fe, NM 87504
800-849-8751
http://www.greenmoney.com

This journal promotes the awareness of socially and environmentally responsible business, investing, and consumer resources. The publisher's goal is to educate and empower individuals and businesses to make informed financial decisions.

More Than Money
71 Junction Square
Concord, MA 01742
978-371-1726
http://www.morethanmoney.org

This quarterly publication is written for people questioning society's assumptions about money, particularly those with inherited or earned wealth who are seeking a more joyful, just, and sustainable world.

Web Sites

The Motley Fool
123 N. Pitt Street
Alexandria, VA 22314
703-838-3665
http://www.fool.com

The Motley Fool is an organization dedicated to educating people about money and finance.

SmartMoney
1755 Broadway, 2nd Floor
New York, NY 10019
800-444-4204
http://www.smartmoney.com

A web site from *SmartMoney,* a financial magazine published jointly by Dow Jones and Hearst that covers all major financial issues.

Resources to Help You Get Organized

Davidson, Jeff. *Breathing Space*. New York: MasterMedia, 1991, 2000. (http://www.breathingspace.com) A guide for people who feel they are drowning in paper and information. Suggests ways to get in control of your space so you can get in control of the rest of your life.

Davidson, Jeff. *The Joy of Simple Living*. Emmaus, PA: Rodale Press, 1999. Focuses on ways to reduce clutter and complication from your life. Takes you drawer by drawer and room by room.

Eisenberg, Ronni, and Kate Kelly. *Organize Your Home! Revised Simple Routines for Managing Your Household*. New York: Hyperion, 1994, 1998. (http://www.reisenberg.com) Provides information on getting your house in order, including how to organize valuable papers.

Homefile Publishing
1290 Bay Dale Drive, Suite 355
Arnold, MD 21012
800-695-3453
http://www.organizerkits.com

This company sells helpful organizational materials for filing financial information.

Morgenstern, Julie. *Organizing from the Inside Out*. New York: Henry Holt/Owl, 1998. (http://www.juliemorgenstern.com) A method of organizing based on your personal goals, habits, and psychological needs.

The National Association of Personal Financial Advisors (NAPFA)
3250 N. Arlington Heights Road, Suite 109
Arlington Heights, IL 60004
800-366-2732
http://www.napfa.org

This organization offers referrals to fee-only financial planners in all areas of the country.

Yager, Jan. *Creative Time Management for the New Millennium.* Stamford, CT: Hannacroix Creek Books, Inc., 1999. (http://www .janyager.com) A time management guide that recognizes the hectic world we live in and gives specific advice on how to be more effective and creative in managing your time.

Chapters Five and Six

Books

Bolen, Jean Shinoda, MD. *Urgent Message from Mother: Gather the Women, Save the World*, Berkeley, CA: Red Wheel Weiser, 2005.

Bolen, Jean Shinoda, MD. *The Millionth Circle: How to Change Ourselves and the World.* Berkeley, CA: Conari Press, 1999. Dr. Bolen wrote this book "to inspire women to form circles." She believes that the movement to form women's circles will change the world and bring humanity into a postpatriarchal era.

Cameron, Julia. *The Vein of Gold.* New York: Jeremy P. Tarcher, 1996. Expanding on the idea of a spiritual DNA, Cameron offers readers a way to explore and elicit the emergence of their own creativity.

Fardelmann, Charlotte. *Nudged by the Spirit: Stories of People Responding to the Still, Small Voice of God.* Pendle Hill, PA: Pendle Hill Publications, 2001. Stories of the dreams that have come to fruition with the help of seed money from the Lyman Fund.

Gary, Tracy, and Melissa Kohner. *Inspired Philanthropy*. Berkeley, CA: Chardon Press, 1998, second edition San Francisco: Jossey-Bass, 2002. A workbook designed to help you find your passion and to identify ways to make personal philanthropic contributions.

Hunt, Helen LaKelly. *Faith and Feminism: A Holy Alliance*. Atria Books/Simon & Schuster, 2004. Stories of five exceptional spiritual women living their truth.

Jones, Laurie Beth. *The Path: Creating Your Mission Statement for Work and for Life*. New York: Hyperion, 1996. A simplified way to define your life's mission and develop a clear declaration.

Shaw, Sondra C. and Martha A. Taylor. *Reinventing Fundraising, Realizing the Potential of Women's Philanthropy*. San Francisco: Jossey-Bass, 1995.

Twist, Lynne, *The Soul of Money, Transforming Your Relationship with Money and Life*. New York: WW Norton and Company, 2003.

Magazines

Faith@Work
Faith at Work
106 E. Broad Street, Suite B
Falls Church, VA 22046-4501
703-237-3426
http://www.FaithAtWork.com

A Christian magazine with practical information about faith, family, community, and work life.

Lapis
The New York Open Center, Inc.
83 Spring Street
New York, NY 10012

http://www.lapismagazine.org

An online magazine concerned with the inner meaning of contemporary life.

YES
Positive Futures Network
PO Box 10818
Bainbridge Island, WA 98110
206-842-0216

http://www.yesmagazine.org

A magazine devoted to stories of good and creative events in the world—truly good news.

Study Groups

Institute of Noetic Sciences
101 San Antonio Road
Petaluma, CA 94952
707-775-3500
http://www.noetic.org

Its journal chronicles trends, new ideas, and data in the interdisciplinary field of conscious research.

Marion Foundation
3 Barnabas Road
Marion, MA 02738-1421
508-748-0816
http://www.marionfoundation.org

An organization providing workshops and monthly mailings about philanthropy, alternative medicine, and global spiritual and economic concerns.

Ministry of Money
11315 Neelsville Church Road
Germantown, MD 20876
301-428-9560
http://www.ministryofmoney.org

An excellent resource for people on a Christian money journey, offering programs, events, and a newsletter.

Interfaith Groups

The Council for a Parliament of the World's Religions
70 E. Lake Street, Suite 205
Chicago, IL 60601
312-629-2990
http://www.cpwr.org

The Forge Institute
383 Broadway
Hastings-on-Hudson, NY 10706
914-478-7802
http://www.theforge.org

The Temple of Understanding
720 Fifth Avenue, 16th Floor
New York, NY 10019
212-246-2746
http://www.templeofunderstanding.org

United Religions Initiative
PO Box 29242
San Francisco, CA 94129
415-561-2300
http://www.uri.org

Women's Donor Network
1804 Embarcadero Road, Suite 200
Palo Alto, CA 94303
650-855-9600
http://www.womendonors.org

Women's Funding Network
1375 Sutter Street, Suite 406
San Francisco, CA 94109
415-441-0706
http://www.wfnet.org

Women's Perspective
421 Meadow Street
Fairfield, CT 06430
203-336-2238
http://www.womensperspective.org

Women's Philanthropy Institute
Center on Philanthropy, Indiana University
550 West North Street, Suite 301
Indianapolis, IN 46202-3272
317-274-4200
http://www.women-philanthrophy.org

About the Authors

Rosemary C. Williams is the director of Women's Perspective, based in Fairfield, Connecticut. The organization provides opportunities for women to explore their relationship with money from a spiritual perspective. In this capacity she designs and conducts retreats and workshops across the country and leads traveling workshops to economically deprived countries. As a financial planner and former banker, she has combined her professional training with her spiritual life. This synthesis of financial know-how and spiritual belief has led her to participate in the initiation of community development projects in Haiti and Kenya. She lives in Connecticut and is the mother of five grown children and the grandmother of three incredible grandchildren.

Joanne Kabak is a journalist and author based in Westport, Connecticut. She has collaborated on four books and is widely published in newspapers and magazines. She has an MBA from Columbia University and practiced as a CPA in New York City before starting her own writing and consulting business, Clarity Communications. Her web site is www.joannekabak.com.

About Women's Perspective

Women's Perspective scheduled its first events in the early 1980s in recognition of the fact that women brought a unique voice to the subjects of money, faith, and economic justice. We continue to design and facilitate retreats and workshops that provide space for women to explore their relationship with money. We offer a safe place to learn, think, journal, and examine the impact money has on our spiritual life, self-image, family, relationships, and community.

In addition to retreats and workshops, we offer transformational trips to economically deprived countries, such as Haiti, Guatemala, and Kenya. On these trips we develop relationships with women of the country we visit in order to understand their lives and share our friendship, experiences, and resources. Through the generosity of foundations and individual donors, we have started several international initiatives. These include economic partnerships with women's groups in Haiti, the establishment of community radio stations, advanced educational opportunities for Haitian women, marketing the products of an embroidery cooperative, and ongoing financial support for a neighborhood health clinic. In recent years we have been offering workshops to HIV/AIDS widows in Kisumu, Kenya, and initiating relationships and projects with widows and orphans in the same area. We have nurtured many friendships across cultural boundaries and continue to transform our own lives as well as those of the women we meet in our travels.

As we deepen our commitment to working with money and spirituality, we encourage women to come together in small circles to continue sharing their experiences related to money, faith, and values.

To get more information, register for a retreat, become part of a local group, or start a study group, you can reach us in the following ways:

On the Web: http://www.womensperspective.org

By phone: 203-336-2238

By fax: 203-336-2240

By e-mail: info@womensperspective.org

By mail: 421 Meadow Street
Fairfield, CT 06430

48749500R10121

Made in the USA
Lexington, KY
12 January 2016